D1074368

. . . The New Professors

. . . The New Professors

COMPILED, WITH A PREFACE, BY

ROBERT O. BOWEN

Holt, Rinehart and Winston, Inc.

NEW YORK

Published simultaneously in Canada

FIRST EDITION

Printed in the United States of America

Library of Congress Catalog Number: 60-6765

. . . Acknowledgment

THIS IS TO ACKNOWLEDGE my considerable debt to the following, especially for their assistance in locating certain of the authors: Professor George Bluestone and Professor Jerome Beaty of the University of Washington, Robert B. Davis of the Prentice Hall Company, and Henry Carlisle and William Hackett, Jr., of Rinehart & Company.

Robert O. Bowen

. . . *Editor's Preface*

DURING the past few years, and especially since Sputnik I, an entire literature has been produced on the American university and the American professor. Any back-country commentator can now explain that in contrast to other professional people the professor is underpaid, that Science faculties are in short supply, or that there is too little respect for Humanities professors. *The American Legion Magazine* has voiced complaints against the radicalism of professors; meanwhile the American Association of University Professors has taken an ultra-conservative stand on the problem of faculty tenure regulations. Within the profession, partisan causes have flared up: *progressive education* or as its opponents might say, "training for delinquency"; *practical engineering courses* or say, "trade schools"; even the literary critics express major schisms in debating whether literature is sociology or art, revelation or parlor game.

Out of the statistics, the opinion, and the prejudice several anomalous images of the current professor have arisen: The Ph. D. Quiz Kid, The Tweedy Defector, The Crewcut Scientist, and, since he has never gone away, Old Mr. Chipps mumbling Liberal platitudes beneath his mane of white hair. *The New Professors* is a symposium by professors from various fields, none of whom ultimately fits a stereotype. As one contributor suggests, graduate schools are not cooky cutters that stamp out exactly the same product at each stroke. In this symposium we have tried to get beyond the Hollywood image and the *Little Orphan Annie* image and *The New York Times* image of the professor and to show what the university profession looks like to the insider.

In order to keep *The New Professors* spontaneous, we led the contributors with only a few questions: How did you get into the university? and: What are you doing there? Thus what the essays offer is fresh from the spring, as it were, and not doctored by a series of editors and a publisher. The cross section included is obviously not statistically accurate; after all, nine men hardly represent the entire university profession. We have included, for instance, no woman professor though there are many; again we have no Negro professor; and we lack a Dental Hygienist and a Forester. Given sufficient space, we would have included these and others. The basis of our choice was simple. We invited younger men who were effective in their particular fields and who represented important aspects of academic work or campus life. We also selected representatives of certain small but important minorities. For example, we picked a political exile in Chandler Davis because the possibility of exile has been a very great influence on the conduct of most professors in the past decade or so. And we have in Mr. Echols of Phillips Exeter Academy a voluntary exile, one who left university life in order to find an academic haven in a prep school. Numerous specifications can be seen aside from these two: The Chemist, The Psychologist, The Administrator, The Liberal, and so on.

Our choice was of competent and productive men who are in some way altering their campuses or influencing their fields, whether greatly or not. To be quite bald about the matter, we selected men who are known to their peers, nationally to some extent, as "good" men. Because we wanted men whose careers are still being shaped, we avoided those who have already been elevated to the atypical heights of popular national eminence. As a result the contributors are such as any reader might find on any campus. *The New Professors* offers a fair sample of the men who do the teaching and the committee work, who select the textbooks, and who are shaping their departments for the future. One is a Department Chairman, one a Director of Freshman English, and one the Co-ordinator of a Counseling Center; one is a full professor, three are associate professors, three assistant professors, and one is still an instructor. One is no longer a member of a school or university.

Many of the important differences between these younger men and their predecessors are concealed or remain vague. It is easy enough to note that fewer Phi Beta Kappa members now wear the fraternity key. To define the social attitudes of the profession at large is quite another problem. Still, facts can be pointed out where they cannot be thoroughly explained. As recently as World War II, when many of our contributors were themselves students, the professor was often a man with a private income. At some Ivy League universities such a man was usual. Generally, too, the professor was the son of a professional or landed family. A joke is still current about a well-known academician who was dropped from the Stanford faculty in the 'twenties when it was discovered that he was trying to live on his salary; and it is still true at some Ivy League institutions that English instructors earn less annually than the local ditchdiggers do.

A generation or more ago the professional attitude among academic people was more like that of today's medical men. Once a man was appointed to a faculty in those earlier times, he was looked upon as a permanent member, as though he had married in. The struggles for power and position were not for survival in the institution but rather for eminence, for perhaps a famous chair. Today the competition among faculty people on certain campuses threatens to give the Liberal Arts a worse name among intellectuals than that assigned to Madison Avenue. As several contributors point out, the most painful pressures on the professor today frequently come from within the profession.

On academic freedom or any other matter, though, the contributors fall into one common generality: they differ. Where some note severe limits in free expression, others speak out with no concern at all for censure. Though several comment on salary, this does not appear to be a serious problem to the majority. To judge from the widely divergent philosophies of Sociologist Emerson and Chemist Young, American professors continue to express a hopefully broad range of thought. The lack of regularity shown here suggests a variety of opinion that some observers have feared no longer exists in the American university.

Idealism, whether religious as with Professor Young or more nearly ethical as with Professor Welch, is an important element throughout the symposium. The idealism expressed in the essays, however, is not in the traditional academic form.

It is immensely more practical than the lofty but unarticulated notions that caused the ivory-tower cliché. From essay to essay there is a note of self-respect through competence of craft, through actually being able to do rather than merely to teach. This is a new note in the academy. Whatever teachers may actually have been in the past, they have not always thought of themselves as doers. Possibly the major distinction between an older generation of academics and the current one is that the new man does his professing with more relevance to the world off-campus.

The real intent of *The New Professors,* though, is not to offer conclusions, even such vague ones as this; instead, it is to give an inside view of the university as a way of life. The symposium shows how professors see themselves, what they find important in their work, how they came to be professors. In short, it shows what sort of men they are personally, beyond the statistics and the graduate degrees and the Phi Beta Kappa keys.

Robert O. Bowen
Seattle, Washington
September, 1959

. . . Contents

Contents

. . . The New Professors

. . . *What's the Image?*

RICHARD E. WELCH, JR.

MY WIFE and I have a number of friends who live and work in New York City. Though at one time they sported a variety of occupations, they now all acknowledge an affiliation with The Communications Field. As the town of Easton, Pennsylvania, where we live, is but seventy miles from New York, we can expect several visits from these communicators during the course of an average year. They enjoy getting away from the city and breathing again the country air. Easton is a city of some sixty thousand.

I would not wish to convey the impression that we do not appreciate their visits, for, in measure, we do. It is always a bit disturbing to me, however, to see what a strange idea they entertain of a college professor, which I happen to be, and of a cozy little college town, which the city of Easton is not. They would not admit, of course, to entertaining an idea. Rather I find that what everyone and everything now "projects" is an Image. The Image which they entertain of a college professor is that of someone who has decided not to enter the race, but rather to live a life of leisurely calm, chatting with a few students, browsing through a few books, and generally having a soporific time of it while his more aggressive companions exhaust themselves in the rat race of the Communications Industry.

It is usual to express a certain amount of envy about the professorial life; indeed, on occasion there is sometimes a reckless statement to the effect that if the pace in New York becomes any more frantic, they might very well throw in the sponge and retire to the professorial pastures themselves. If I find this in any way irritating, it is perhaps because such remarks usually fall on those days when I am a little weary from three lectures straight, a senior-thesis conference, a department meeting and the grading of what appears, for the moment, to be the most illegible set of blue books ever perpetrated by mankind. Or the conversation will take this turn during that least childlike hour of the day when guests wish a touch more ice water while four hungry children imply that supper must be brought forth immediately.

Our New York friends, incidentally, do not have children. Rather this year they seem to be breeding finches.

On a recent visit this spring by a New York couple and their finch, "Gomorrah," my vocabulary was enlarged by the discovery that the coalescence of two Images makes The Picture. Both of these friends work "in" Television—somewhere on the fringes of *Omnibus*—and as we talked I had a rather uneasy sensation that we were blocking out a scene:

"What do you teach, now? I always forget."

I tell them I teach American history.

"I *hated* American history. The only history I ever felt sympatico with was Medieval. All those wonderful kings with their crazy names."

"Tell me, fellow, just what do you try and project? What's the image?"

"And tell us about the college here, about Lafayette. Not the statistics, but the flavor."

"Yes, give us The Picture. You know, how do you and Lafayette fit in? What's the total image? You know, The Picture."

The value of conversations such as this is that, apart from their intrinsic excitement, they do have a nagging way of forcing a certain amount of self-examination and nostalgia upon one.

Later that evening, unfortunately much later, I got to wondering just what was my Image and that of the college where I taught. I also got to wondering just how it happened that our respective images had meshed to form a picture, be it capitalized or not. The last thought was rather the easier to follow in any consecutive fashion. Indeed, as I reviewed what on an application form I would call my "academic vita," I became nearly convinced that it was fated that the Image of a round-faced apprentice historian named Welch and that of a men's college of some 1500 students and 137 faculty members named Lafayette converge—to the benefit and satisfaction of the apprentice historian.

I decided at the age of thirteen that I was going to be a history teacher and nothing else. This was not particularly unusual, for at that age I knew everything and was positive about even more. The distinction of that decision was that it was the only one I made at that time which I have not subsequently found to be impossible, erroneous, or both.

I was then a freshman in the public high school in Newburyport, Massachusetts, and an interest in history which I had entertained since the age of nine was being furthered by a course in World History given by a lady of great exuberance and charm. As the lady was well over sixty, I refuse to believe there was anything involved here but what my friends today might call "excellent communication contact."

It is, of course, currently popular to damn the public high school as an example of educational democracy gone sour. Without making any pretense at posing as an expert on secondary-school education today, I would insist that some twenty years ago it was possible to obtain at least in one high school a group of courses and teachers that furnished an excellent background for college. There was a good deal of peripheral activity at N. H. S., surely—at one time I was a proud member of seven clubs, ranging from the Pasty Hooding, a dramatic outfit of sorts, to the Camera Club, which I do not recall ever met—but the student body did not take any of it too seriously. Of the four scholastic curricula, two were college preparatory, and these offered as wide a range of courses as the average preparatory school. True, the classes were considerably larger than those in the average preparatory school; surely we had insufficient practice with the "hourly quiz" and the "three-hour exam," which perform, perhaps unfortunately, so crucial a function in college grading, but I would guess that the interest and ability of our teachers were not inferior to any but the very top preparatory schools. There was one teacher who had an unfortunate habit on Monday mornings of giving an extra study period during the class hour, but by and large the faculty were professionally competent, conscientious, and—considering the amount of cafeteria notices and other administrative rigmarole they had to wade through—amazingly agreeable.

From Newburyport High School, I went to Dartmouth College. My years at Dartmouth were split by forty-five months in the army during World War II, so this was, in a sense, a rather schizophrenic experience. As a freshman I went out "heeling" for a wide variety of organizations and became deeply enthralled with the Dartmouth ideal of the well-rounded individual. So deeply enthralled as a matter of fact that I flunked a so-called "gut" entitled Graphics I. Possessed of a roommate who was an embryo Big Man on Campus, I had a delightful year, the only parts of which I remember with any real clarity are a term paper on the social novels of Benjamin Disraeli and a trip to the Harvard Stadium where the Dartmouth freshman class waved white handkerchiefs across to the Harvard side at the end of a special and labored cheer, thereby signifying our undying conviction that all Harvard men were effete if not worse.

I came back to Hanover after the war, a very purposeful and single-minded "grind." I wished to do three years in two by attending college the year round, and I wished to get sufficient grades so I could attend a good graduate school. That these years were even more satisfying than my freshman year, despite this rather narrow purposefulness, was due solely to the Dartmouth history department.

It was not a brilliant department, in the Harvard definition of the adjective. Various of its members had surely "published," some of them in quite distinguished fashion, but it was primarily a "teaching department" and an unusually successful one. Though I had long professed to myself a great interest in history, it was not until I was a Dartmouth history major that I had any idea of what history was and was not.

Two courses especially stand out in my memory: one a single semester course on the types and varieties of historical writing and the methodology of the historian; the other, a one-semester course devoted exclusively to a Senior Thesis.

In the latter course, one was assigned to that member of the department whose special field of research best fitted the student's topic. As I had chosen to write on Caleb Cushing and the Treaty of Wanghia, I was assigned to Professor Herbert Hill, who gave the course in American diplomatic history. As I look back now, he did a remarkable job of keeping me in fairly close rein while forcing me to stumble ahead under my own steam.

There is today a great deal of chatter about the need to make college less of a teaching institution and more an emporium for self-learning, with the teachers huddled in the wings and the student blazing ahead on his own, with only the help of Fowler, Roget, and certain paperbacks. All such talk seems to me to pose a dichotomy that need not exist. To say that a professor "gives" a course and that a student "takes" it need in no wise deny to the student the ability to think creatively or, indeed, work like fury. The ability to listen to a lecture, understand it, take notes on it, and argue about it in the next class session is not a particularly shameful talent.

If memory serves me correctly, I never took a history course at Dartmouth that was *purely* lecture, class discussion, library research, or student symposium. Rather there was an appreciation on the part of the department that no single "kind" of classroom plan or technique was advisable for every topic or aspect of the course. There was no great concern with methodology; simply an unremitting effort to get the material across in as coherent, meaningful and interesting a manner as possible. I suppose it was all very old-fashioned, but I remember it with great pleasure. I have, indeed, often thought that if what her catalogue calls The Dartmouth Experience is to be symbolized by any one thing, it should not be the Winter Carnival, the Snow Bunny, the Lone Pine, or even white-columned Dartmouth Row, but rather by a faculty that refused to talk much of the Student-Teacher Relationship and thus succeeded in that relationship extremely well.

From Hanover to Harvard Square is not geographically much of a distance, but from the rather clubby atmosphere of the Dartmouth History Department to the rather arctic atmosphere of the Harvard Graduate School of Arts and Sciences is quite a journey. I spent four years at Harvard, two of them consumed with course work, the other two with the research and writing of a doctoral dissertation. In those four years, I came to know four of my professors slightly, and only one, Professor Merk who directed my dissertation, well. I suppose the moral to that rather maudlin statistic is that I did not go to the Harvard Graduate School to eat and drink with its distinguished faculty but to study under them. On the latter score, I owe Harvard a great deal; though when I am asked whether I cheer for Dartmouth or Harvard when these two titans clash athletically, I cannot help but find the question absurd.

There is, of course, no originality in the thought that there are both great values and definite disadvantages in doing graduate study at a large university, but like most truisms, it is true. If one does not care for the occasional sensation of being a lost soul in the catacombs of scholarship, one should avoid working in Widener Library. If one is convinced that a distinguished scholar will always deliver a stimulating lecture, one should avoid Harvard University. On the other hand, if one wishes to study the techniques of historical scholarship under the tutelage of some of the most able, knowledgeable and technically proficient historians in the world, one could perhaps do no better than Harvard.

I suppose I gained at Harvard two rather essential things. One, a union card so I could have a chance to practice at long last the profession I had so early chosen. The other was the opportunity to do research under the gimlet eye and fatherly hand of Frederick Merk, the man to whom I am most indebted for whatever I know of the burdens and excitements of historical scholarship. The absolute personification of scholarly conscience, he forced me to a thousand tasks of research that I felt to be utterly unnecessary, to countless revisions of style which I knew to be necessary but did not care to bother with, and most of all set for me a goal of excellence which I shall never achieve and for which I shall always be grateful. If when preparing a lecture today I am tempted to slip in some half-remembered fact or anecdote, it is the conscience of Merk, not of Welch, that propels me to "check all the available sources, and then go on and look further."

During my last year at Harvard, I attended my first American Historical Association meeting. These AHA meetings are a strong combination of erudite assembly and slave market. Half the population is listening earnestly to various papers and new "Findings," the other and younger half is desperately roaming the lobby, foyer and corridor in an effort to accidentally come upon some departmental chairman who might have a job to offer. Largely by means of such a stroll and the earnest efforts of Professor Merk I obtained my first job, a substitute, one-year appointment as an instructor in history at Colgate University.

Apart from convincing me that I enjoyed the role of college teacher, my stay at Colgate was too short to give me much idea of either that institution or the proper Image for a college professor.

My next appointment was for a much longer period,

and was one of the more interesting episodes of my academic career to date. For five years I served as an assistant professor of history at The Virginia Military Institute, and thereby enjoyed an experience novel on several accounts. For one thing it was the first time I had ever been in a Southern college or military school or an institution where the emphasis was clearly on engineering sciences rather than the liberal-arts curriculum. It was also the first time that I had been associated with a college where the members of the faculty automatically referred to members of the colored race as "nigras" and where the members of the faculty were, without exception, mannerly and courteous in the extreme on all occasions.

There is, of course, a small body of literature devoted to the Southern military college. This literature falls into two chief categories. The college is made out to be a sort of Peck's Bad Boy prep school where commandants are forever foiled from discovering that the dates are in the barracks (but only to help the dumb but jovial boy from Mississippi with his chemistry), or the college is made out to be a sort of cesspool of depravity whose true founder should be the Marquis de Sade not Stonewall Jackson. From my experience at V.M.I., both of these characterizations are equally erroneous. As the cadets whom I knew made little of the intellectual attributes of their dates, I sincerely doubt that much time was spent on the "hops" weekends with chemistry texts. Nor did I see any signs that the Parade Ground was Port Said in disguise.

I rather suspect that most of the exposés on life at Virginia Military Institute are written by individuals whose acquaintance with the institution is of a week's duration. If this is the case, their misconceptions are easily understood. During my first week of teaching in the South I recall entertaining the thought that I was going quietly mad to the tempo of a big bass drum beating out the thumping rhythms of the Spirit Song. I was not used to having students march into class, or to seeing them stand at attention until I gave the order, "Seats, gentlemen." I was somewhat thrown by seeing the freshmen—or better, "Rats"—humbly hugging the walls as they marched down the corridors, and actually confused when upon glancing in at the Mess Hall one day I saw the same "Rats" eating a Square Meal, bringing their food from plate to mouth by means of a severely rectangular motion.

Indeed, at the end of the first week I was convinced that the student accepted by The Virginia Military Institute was a unique character who had little or nothing in common with his civilian counterpart. I was ready to believe that the chief academic occupation was shining brass, that the idea of addressing the Dean of Faculty as General would forever strike me as Chaplinesque, and that I would never as a point of honor condescend to call the campus, "the Post."

Before the first year was up, however, I was enjoying—if somewhat confusedly—life on the Post, and was reluctantly accepting the realization that young men, eighteen to twenty-one, are pretty much the same at any college, whether their uniform be garrison caps and high tops or beanies and carefully dirtied bucks. If there was to my prejudiced way of thinking too great an emphasis on military decorum and the general externals, I was nevertheless gradually forced to admit that despite all the shining of brass, the right obliques, the constant military formations, and the hooplah of the "Rat Line," lessons were prepared; indeed, in many cases prepared with an exhibition of individual imagination that defied the conformity of the long gray line. One of my more vivid recollections is of a First Classman who, after zealously "chewing out" a Rat for daring to walk diagonally across the corridor outside my office, then entered that office, saluted smartly, and turned in an excellent paper entitled, "The Persecution of Pacifists in World War I: The Stain on America's Shield."

The epitome of such a college as I am describing is the Honor System and the Honor Court. Here is concentrated the essential paradox of an institution which attempts to straddle the academic life and the military system.

Every incoming Rat learned that there were three offenses which so violated the code of the cadet that anyone suspected of committing any of them would be brought before the Student Honor Court and, if found guilty, would be expelled from the Institute. These offenses were Making a False Official Statement, Cheating and Stealing. Any cadet who had proper cause to believe that one of his colleagues had committed any of these crimes had the positive duty to report him to the Honor Court committee. If this was a violation of the "no tattling" precept of the playground, it was a purposeful one. Not only could the Honor System not operate successfully without such an arrangement, but every freshman was instilled with the idea that one's duty to the Honor of the Cadet Corps was greater than any sentiments of personal friendship.

The trials of the Honor Court were studiously fair, with the accused given every chance of proving his innocence. A possibly necessary part of the System, however, was the severity of the punishment. Not only was the cadet expelled, but his dishonorable conduct was publicized in what to a civilian-minded soul like myself seemed unnecessarily cruel fashion. As the trials were held at night, the assembly drum would usually beat at two in the morning. The entire corps of cadets would hastily assemble along the outdoor balconies of the barracks, every man facing the center of the court yard. There the drum would roll again, the culprit's name and his offense be announced, and the cadet in question stripped of his insignia. This process was called "drumming out." A cadet who was expelled in this manner was dead so far as his former classmates were concerned. It was understood that he would never again step foot on the Post so long as he lived.

I have gone on in this lengthy fashion about the Honor System at V.M.I., for it seems to me that it is representative of both the worst and the best of a military college. In its inflexibility and military fanfare, it is possibly symbolic of other aspects of such an education. Yet, too, it represents a firm belief that conscience as well as competence should be taught and that principles are not only to be mouthed but adhered to. If it smacks a little of Tyrone Power in India, it also carries with it perhaps the most palatable aspect of the Legend of the Old South—the notion that there are certain standards of honor to which every man owes undeviating obedience. How best to inculcate such standards of conduct remains, of course, an open question. Basic to a military—or an ecclesiastical—education is the idea that if an individual is forced to adhere rigidly to a prescribed code during "the formative years," that code becomes a permanent part of his make-up and throughout his later life he will adhere to it voluntarily. The fundamental assumption is that strict discipline makes eventually for self-discipline.

I would testify that for some it surely does. The faculty at V.M.I. were very largely Institute graduates, and for the most part they proved the point that for some young men, the frenetic discipline of the Rat Line was conducive to the development of character as well as the acquisition of knowledge. I would not set this faculty up as pioneers on the boundaries of knowledge in their respective fields, but a group of professors more deserving of the term gentlemen it would be hard to find. I came and left a Damnyankee in the eyes of most, if not all, and yet I can never recall an incident when a single colleague was not amiable as well as mannerly.

Actually the gentlemanly calm that pervaded the history department was somewhat deceptive. Though it was considered improper to make a great deal of fuss over it, most of the members of that department had their own research project on which they labored with reasonable diligence. The Civil War and Reconstruction man was, indeed, a scholar of solid and growing reputation.

I am not able to think of the Institute today in exactly the terms that one of its graduates would—certain that its Corps of Cadets embodied all American virility, that its faculty comprised all that was true and blue of the professorial profession. Rather I think of it as one of the finest examples of a type of education in which I can see very real merit for certain young men, but not for the majority. For the majority of young men I believe a civilian college which places large emphasis on the Liberal Arts is likely to be most rewarding—viewed in terms of knowledge gained either of subject or of self.

As I am currently employed by such a college, I seem finally to have come to the subject of Lafayette and the merging of the Images.

For me the appeal of Lafayette is composed of a rather wide variety of items, some of them seemingly trite, but in the sum, not unimportant. For one thing it is not too large; only fifteen hundred students. Neither the student nor the teacher need feel lost in the crowd. For another, it is a men's college. I am quite willing to admit that women are generally more attractive than men, and possibly even brighter. I refuse to believe, however, that they are as easily taught. I do not base that peevish contention on classroom experience. Because of its size and sexually homogeneous population, there is in fact something that could be—but fortunately is not—called the Lafayette Community. By that I mean that there is a certain sense of common identity between students and teachers. This does not collapse into the Togetherness fandango which you sometimes get in ultra-progressive girls' colleges, where the students vote on who shall become departmental chairman. Rather the aim is a sort of balance, with the professor expected to give top priority to his students but not to act the nursemaid or chaplain.

In the same connection, Lafayette aims at a balance between the professor's obligations to his students and to his discipline. Though it is understood that each faculty member is primarily hired to teach, there is nonetheless a very real effort made to stimulate research and afford the teacher-scholar those essentials for scholarly activity—time and money. It is not unnatural for a college to encourage research and publication on the part of its faculty, of course. Faculty publication is assuredly good advertising for the college. At Lafayette, however, there is, I believe, an honest effort to encourage research and writing for the still more valid reason that the teacher who has quit as a scholar is most likely on his way to becoming deadwood as a teacher. In this sense, it is rather more the research project that a college such as Lafayette is interested in than publication *per se.* There is surely no grinding demand to publish so many pages or ounces within the calendar year. Neither is there any idea that publication in itself connotes brilliance so blinding that it must be rewarded by professorial rank by Saturday next.

Finally, there is an attempt to achieve a balance within the Lafayette curriculum between the how-to courses and those that might properly be labeled, why-so or even so-what. Though a school with a long Liberal Arts tradition, Lafayette today sports a strong engineering curriculum as well as a wide variety of majors in the humanities and the social and "pure" sciences. None of its students, however, really succeeds in escaping the Liberal Arts tradition. There is a continuous effort to cross divisional lines and a very real conviction on the part of the professors in "engineering," as well as in "fine arts," that no man can be educated by the slide rule alone.

If I appear here a little extreme in my praise, it is not because I am under the misapprehension that Lafayette is shorthand for Academic Valhalla, or that all of its ideals have been realized or its desire to balance teaching and research, technical courses and the humanities is always and automatically successful. Rather what impresses me chiefly is the unanimity among the faculty as to the general, over-all goals which a college such as Lafayette should be striving for. Disputes as to methods, ways and means, and committee assignments there are, and plenty. But by and large there is common agreement on the essentials. And chief among those essentials is a belief that Lafayette is not a research university, a municipal junior college, or an adult education center. Rather it aspires to excellence within its particular sphere: the relatively small men's college that emphasizes teaching without neglecting research; that appreciates the demands of modern technology but refuses to forego its Liberal Arts heritage.

The profession of college teaching is naturally not without its irritations at Lafayette or anywhere else. There are days when one is convinced that the best thing that could happen for education is for the mimeograph machine in the Administration Building to disintegrate from overwork. There are more days when one is convinced that he is the only professorial soul in existence who does not purposely try to elongate a drawn-out committee session. Every lining has its blemish, of course, and at Lafayette the interest and concern of the faculty with the curriculum and student body has the drawback of inducing a proliferation of committees. A faculty that wishes to play a properly formative role in the development of college educational policy must, of course, make studies and dig facts. There is embodied here, however, a definite danger. A committee is the normal instrument for a study. So that as much diversity of opinion as possible can be represented, the committee should be good-sized. A committee too large to be really effective necessitates a subcommittee. And away you go. It is possible at Lafayette, as at most colleges, for a professor of some years' standing to be on as many as four "major" committees, and have as many as eight hours a week snatched from the time that he might have given his students or devoted to his personal research. I am sure there is a Malthusian law to be discovered somewhere with respect to the almost automatic proliferation of committees and committee assignments in a college, or at the very least some sort of geometric ratio.

Another querulous complaint one can make of any small, Eastern, private men's college is that it does not pay its teachers enough. Lafayette has in recent years made rather exceptional improvement on this score, however, and the yearly increase that once was referred to slightingly has developed into a rather healthy boost. By and large there is an effort at Lafayette both to raise minimum salaries and obtain a broader spread within the various fields of rank. In the latter connection the idea is to emphasize more "the merit increase," and recognize the inevitable variations in quality of performance between one teacher and another.

There will perhaps never be a time in the history of Lafayette or any other privately financed institution when salaries will be sufficiently high, at least in the eyes of their recipients, but one thing does much to counterbalance this fact. It is usually at the private college that the teacher is most certain of academic freedom both in terms of such technical matters as tenure and, more importantly, in the classroom itself. The knowledge that you are accorded the trust to say what you will and arrange your courses in any way you see fit is something more than a "fringe" benefit, and one it would be difficult to put a price upon. Such academic freedom affords for the teacher the same sort of stimulation and self-respect which an open-stacks library policy grants the student. Both are an integral part of the Lafayette Image.

The feature of that image most familiar to me is, of course, the History Department. It is, I believe, typical of the college at large. Relatively small—it has but six members—it has what I think is a fairly outstanding undergraduate course offering. There is no attempt to confuse Lafayette with a graduate school, nor any attempt to make of every History major a professional historian. The aim is to give the student a greater understanding of the way in which various nations, regions and institutions have evolved in time, rather than an expert mastery in the evaluation of primary sources and historical artifacts. There is, however, an honors program which affords those students who do desire to go on to graduate school a rather substantial, if necessarily elementary, education in the tools and techniques of historical scholarship.

It was primarily from the History Department that I tried to "project" for my New York friends an image of the Lafayette Professor. For their better orientation, I initially emphasized that among my immediate colleagues there was not one who is absent-minded; there was not one who could be labeled a fuddy-dud inhabitant of an ivory tower; there were several who might well be called charming—whatever that adjective is supposed to connote—but none who could be labeled, "a charming old codger." Moreover, there were none who exemplified the old Shavian slam that teachers are embittered souls who because they are unable to do anything insist upon the right to teach everyone everything. Indeed, when it comes to dividing the costs of a small impromptu coffee club, I am convinced that several of my departmental colleagues would have done brilliantly in Wall Street.

Well, if they are not cartoon characters, what are they? What do these professors hope to be and do while resident at the architecturally insane and yet strangely attractive campus at Lafayette? These laboriously rhetorical questions can perhaps best be answered by a few examples.

One member of the department teaches several courses in the early period of American history, edits an excellent historical journal, and is currently working on a paper dealing with the limitations of educational TV. This breadth of interest is reflected in the man's teaching and in his near-continuous afternoon conferences with his students. Some of the catalogue descriptions of the courses he teaches might make them appear narrow in scope, but I doubt if there are many students who finish one of those courses without both an appreciation that sloppy writing is a cardinal sin and that no field or variety of history is to be studied in a vacuum.

Across the hall is a professor who is currently writing a book on the Chancellorsville-Gettysburg campaign. He was working away at his manuscript late one afternoon last spring, when a sophomore knocked and asked for a recount on a recently corrected hour exam. The notes were put away, and the student left one hour later, with grade unchanged but a rather better understanding of the Monroe Doctrine and his own limitations.

Another member of the department devoted the evenings of a fortnight to translating a group of German documents, the better to assist a senior who was writing his thesis on Bernstein and the Revisionist Socialists in Germany. This man's particular interest is Italian history.

These examples could be multiplied, but no great purpose would be served. That, perhaps, is the most frustrating part of the professorial life and the task of one who would describe it. Those things which best describe it are meaningful only in their sum and within the context of the particular college, department, student. For one who has never prepared a lecture to be delivered before thirty tremulously blasé freshmen, there is little significance or interest in the fact that such a lecture requires often the consultation of a small ton of old notes and books and some four or five revisions. The average layman will mouth the words, "How I envy you, working with young men in their most formative years!" without the slightest sentiment of envy and little understanding of the obligations and excitements, the discouragements and satisfactions of a teacher's lot. To feel deeply about the importance of something and to be able to communicate that conviction is the satisfaction of this mysterious profession and it is one surprisingly difficult to articulate.

What I suppose most infuriates the average professor is the unspoken assumption of many of his friends that teaching is dull and boring. I have given many dull and boring lectures, but that is the fault of the man not the occupation. No teacher at Lafayette or elsewhere would deny that there are built-in frustrations to the job, days when the most apt illustration falls flat and the seminar group which you had pegged as able or better suddenly seems transfixed in its own stupidity. Frustration, however, is hardly a simile for apathy. There is too much variety in teaching to admit of boredom. In the words of a Lafayette language professor, "Teaching is like bridge. Every hand, every student is different. But teaching is better. Your wife can't play."

Surely teaching in a college such as Lafayette—where one has a chance to be in immediate contact with a wide range of students from different parts of the country, a chance to pursue one's own research under the encouragement of rather than at the insistence of the college, and a chance to experiment with one's courses in an atmosphere of complete academic freedom—is a privilege.

As I reread that line with its rocking-horse style of expression, I am struck with the thought that those aspects of Lafayette which I have been listing as most congenial for a member of its faculty have a rather strong similarity with those features of Dartmouth which, as a student, I most appreciated. This is perhaps only natural. For I rather suspect that all teachers avoid the advice of Thomas Wolfe and do try to go home again. That school or college where first they determined to be teachers or which they found "ideal" is always the one to which they are trying to return. Not that particular college in name, necessarily, but one with the same standards and general priorities. Personally I believe that despite a wide variety of external differences, Dartmouth and Lafayette are cut from the same educational cloth and even, in many respects, to the same pattern.

I failed to give my friends The Big Picture, as I'm sure must be obvious. I found myself reciting in harried fashion a string of anecdotes—some of them most amusing, really, if one knew the cast of characters. They didn't and did not really want to. As they left, one of them breathed a parting bit of self-commiseration:

"How I envy you, old man! Just three hours at the old assembly line tomorrow, and then you're ready to knock off for golf. You look out, fella, the public's going to get wise to you someday. Sweets, watch out for Gomorrah; you're bumping his cage."

Lafayette College

. . . *A Movement West*

ROBERT KATZ

I DID NOT discover that I had any interest in teaching or in academic life until late in my twenties, and then only through a sequence of unrelated circumstances.

It was not the promise of my teens that led me toward this goal. When I noted, on a Christmas card to a former professor, that I was leaving my job in a government laboratory to return to graduate school to get a Ph.D., his kindly note said in reply that it was always a good idea to take more courses. The implication was quite clear.

My private joke about the promise of my teens is not universally shared. During a lull in registration, when faculty members at Kansas State University act as registrar's clerks, I suggested to some of my colleagues that a man approaching his forties, realizing that he is unlikely to achieve any real distinction, sometimes wondered whether he was ever to fulfill the promise of his teens. I had intended the remark to be funny, but instead of generating gales of laughter, it was greeted by pained expressions and asides such as, "We all feel that way sometimes." Rather sharply I became aware that many of these men had always been at the head of their class, and even those that seemed dull and subdued had been salutatorians. Now in my forties, I have no vivid recollection of grade school, of high school, or of college. I rather drifted through those years with no sense of goal or of achievement.

I was born in 1917. My parents were Russian-Jewish immigrants who came to New York City at about the turn of the century. In my school years my parents owned a grocery store, which my father opened at five in the morning and closed at midnight, managing about seven hours of sleep with the aid of a midafternoon nap. His was a daily routine, except for Sunday afternoon, when blue laws demanded that the store be closed. In those adolescent years I was anything but gregarious. A recent newspaper account of some psychological research caught my fancy, for this work reported that scientists display late psychosexual development. It was good to find that I was not unique.

We lived in a working-class neighborhood in the Bronx. Our neighbors were largely Irish, German and Italian immigrants. In accordance with the pedagogy of the 'twenties, I had skipped three semesters by the sixth grade. Whether for this reason, or because most of the kids on my block attended parochial school, I was rarely in the same class as my playmates. For no reason that I now recall I enrolled in a college preparatory course in the neighborhood high school. Looking back, it was a matter of great good fortune that such a curriculum was available, for I found myself taking four years of English and three years of foreign language without conscious planning on my part. I was able to get four years of mathematics, and this was one subject I enjoyed. I took these opportunities for granted, though now I know that educational fashions have changed, and that my own students rarely have such a curriculum offered them. By the time I was in high school, in 1930, the great depression had struck, and our neighborhood felt it keenly. In those years many kids quit school, took out working papers, and found some sort of job.

At sixteen I enrolled in Brooklyn College, a recently organized, tuition-free, municipal college, then housed in rented office buildings in downtown Brooklyn. It took an hour to get to or from school on the subway. I managed to choose this inconvenient location because this school seemed most likely to accept my credentials. In 1933, I could see little point in college, and deferred making application until I could no longer withstand my father's insistence. If there was a guidance program at Brooklyn, it took no notice of me, nor I of it. I took courses as they were required, and found a sophomore required course in physics to have an amalgam of virtues. This course determined my choice of career. Today I count myself fortunate that I was not required to name a curriculum the day I entered college, that I was permitted to flounder around until I had some basis for choosing a field. My own students in Kansas come from different backgrounds, but have many similar problems, especially in making career choices. The numerous psychological tests are incapable of making sharp distinctions. Because of the crowded nature of a technical curriculum, students are forced to elect technical fields early. Not uncommonly, I find students who elect to major in aeronautical engineering because they were good at building model airplanes or who elect civil engineering because the only engineer they ever saw bossed a construction crew, and they like outside work.

As a college junior I had begun to wonder what I was to do when I got my degree. The times were not lush, and by way of insurance I managed to waste the equivalent of nearly a year of college work in a series of dull courses in pedagogy. Several of my classmates were highly regarded. These were the men who left college to take *jobs,* and they loomed large. That summer I patrolled the technical employment agencies, and came to recognize the same well-scrubbed recent graduates filling out application forms in agency after agency to no avail. When I hear my students discuss their employment problems in terms of geography or fringe benefits, I smile and think back to this scramble for fifteen dollars a week. My own classmates were disciples of a newspaper called the *Chief,* which carried announcements of all civil-service examinations, and along with the crowd, I took examinations for everything—elevator operator, laboratory assistant, police clerk, junior physicist—for which I might qualify.

These were gray years. My employment problem was postponed for a year and a half by studying for a master's degree at Columbia University. There were serious difficulties at home. My father had suffered a crippling heart attack that was to kill him at fifty, after a protracted regimen of massage, pill and injection. The year he died one of my many civil-service examinations turned out well. I learned that I led the list for the position of junior physicist. With this assurance that I would find professional employment, I could turn down offers for many menial positions for which I had qualified, and, in September, I found my way to Dayton, Ohio, to go to work for the Army Air Force at Wright Field. I got off the train on Labor Day, 1939, to be assaulted by the headline that Hitler had invaded Poland. I was born in World War I, and had embarked on a career via World War II.

In all I spent seven years at Wright Field, working in two different laboratories. There were a great many reports to write, and in the course of writing them I learned some measure of coherence, for it was a serious deficiency of my education that I was not required to write theme after theme. I learned something of the business of engineering. As a physicist I was able to compete favorably with engineers in the border areas between engineering specialties (as in the circumstance where a metallurgist required some knowledge of electricity), but found myself way behind when the problem lay clearly within conventional engineering bounds.

My first assignment was to become expert in the X-ray inspection of aircraft parts, in the art of taking X-ray pictures and of interpreting them. I bought books on metallurgy, and learned to distinguish between castings and forgings. I bought a set of drawing instruments and an appropriate text and learned what drafting I needed. I visited steel mills and foundries, aircraft factories and engine plants, and acquired a background in aircraft technology under the guidance of two very competent men who were chiefs of the metals unit and the materials laboratory. There was some research to do, and finally I produced the desired specifications for regulating the practice of the art. To the best of my knowledge these are still in use, with slight modification. Interestingly enough, the knowledge gained there was put to use almost as soon as I came to Kansas State, in developing X-ray techniques for finding internal insects in wheat kernels. These techniques are now in world-wide use, and special X-ray equipment for their application is built and sold by Westinghouse, General Electric and other manufacturers. In a sense the Air Force unintentionally subsidized agricultural research, and the state of Kansas gained an unexpected bonus.

For a second assignment I worked with a group attempting to solve an aircraft radio-noise problem called "precipitation static." That group was responsible for the development of the dischargers which hang from the wing tips of most large airplanes. My own contribution included the preparation of the production design of these devices, and the invention and development of other less noticeable gadgets. A great deal of work is involved in developing and producing the most transparently simple technical hardware and I developed a real respect for the work of the ingenious engineer.

At this time I lived in Yellow Springs, Ohio, about fifteen miles from Wright Field, and enjoyed the hospitality of Antioch College, its library, its fine faculty and its student body. My wife is an Antioch alumna, whom I met and married during that time. Concerts, lectures and theatre were available here. Antioch differed from Brooklyn College in many ways. It was small and intimate, where Brooklyn was large and impersonal. Antioch was located in an Ohio village, with a resident student body that came from everywhere in the United States, and went off to co-op jobs every other semester to extend their campus experiences. The student body at Brooklyn came largely from one borough of New York City, gathered by subway and el in the morning and dispersed by the same means in the evening. I think that it was in Yellow Springs that I came to appreciate the work of a college faculty, and to think of this as a possible occupation.

Time passed, and the war was over. I felt a hankering after graduate study, and decided that I must get on with it, for if I got past thirty without getting back to school, I would never make it. As it turned out, I was one of the two old men in graduate study in physics at the University of Illinois. Originally my decision to undertake further study had nothing to do with teaching, but rather stemmed from the observation that I simply did not know enough physics to do most effectively the work I was doing. I fully expected to return to Wright Field, or at least to industry, but without specific reason I slowly drifted toward the notion that I might like a college job.

Perhaps it is fortunate that I did not prepare for the university in any purposeful or directed way, for I suppose if I had been counseled, I might well have been counseled out of teaching. At the University of Illinois, where I went in 1946, graduate students in physics who were considered not to have it were given a pat on the head, a master's degree, and were sent on their way. One short step up and a student was told that he might teach, but that he would never do any research. At the very top of the ladder was academic research in a good school. A physicist at the top of his profession might do some teaching, but only to keep his hand in, and not as his primary concern. My own graduate preparation in physics was for the purpose of doing research, not teaching physics. And though two thirds to three fourths of my time has been spent in teaching, I would not alter this academic preparation. While it would have been difficult and most inefficient to attempt to learn physics for myself, I was able to evolve my own teaching patterns and to reach my own conclusions about the nature of pedagogy and of the university.

It is hard to imagine a subject about which more nonsense is written than the subject of teaching and of teacher preparation. Even bookmen who edit and sell texts in these subjects privately chuckle at a great many of them. I suppose the words that are supposed to tell a concertgoer of the virtues of a symphony, or the comments that are intended to evoke an appreciation for art are also in this nonsense contest. Surely the list of entries in this race includes the jargon that passes for understanding in the social studies, with its tables of statistical how-do-you-do. The latter field might better be rechristened *socistics,* for it consists largely of *soc*ial stat*istics* rather than studies or concepts.

From those who speak in pedagese we hear: The object of the verb *to teach* is *students,* not *subject.* Do not say, "I teach Physics." Instead say, "I teach students." Lecture is bad. Discussion is good. A teacher must have sympathy, understanding, patience and ability to grasp the student's problems, to lead him surely and safely through his intellectual, financial and emotional difficulties. There is no hierarchy of the mind. No subject is better or worse than any other. We must strive to understand each other's problems. Bunk.

The best physics teacher I ever had deliberately avoided all but his own research students. He did so in self-defense. He lectured to graduate classes well over a hundred in size. There was no discussion with him, in class or after. In the two years I attended his lectures I did not exchange a paragraph of conversation with him, though I tried. My long and involved questions in class were answered with a nod of the head, a yes or no, and a patient expression. When one time I got my foot into his office door at the close of a lecture, I was patiently, but ever so clearly, advised that he had a full schedule of research planned for the afternoon. This was the common experience, and commonly we graduate students held him in the highest regard.

Sometimes I am nearly lulled into believing that it might be good for new faculty members to learn something of the structure and organization of the university. But I fear that this knowledge might be most disillusioning and might drive good candidates from the profession. It is better not to be too alert to these questions until the years have tempered one's judgment. It might be disillusioning to learn of college presidents who make impressive speeches they have not written about the importance of education, or that the course of a university is sometimes charted by a politician with an honorary degree, rather than a scholar. Although my opinion is socistically unverified, I retain a bias that a commitment to scholarship, evidenced by its practice, is an essential ingredient in the make-up of a university administrator. From my own experience, a professor is most comfortable and most productive when his department head shares his dedication to their field.

On one occasion I tried to explain my concept of administration to a dean, to no avail. I tried to explain that the productive person in the university is the professor, not the administrator, and not the student. I tried to explain that the successful administrator was one who got his kicks vicariously, from the accomplishments of his faculty. It was his function to hew the wood and draw the water, and to undertake the nonproductive work of running an institution in order to free the faculty for the university's principal job. The burden of a university, the manner in which it fills its role, and its professional reputation depend solely on the faculty which teaches the classes, attracts the students and does the research. These notions seemed to me to be self-evident.

But the dean did not see things my way. In rebuttal I heard how impractical these ideas were. It would be expensive if the college hired clerks to handle the chores of registration, and after all, if the faculty didn't do this, what would they do with their time—paint storm windows? When I argued that faculty should be paid a salary comparable to the income of professional persons in the community, I heard of supply and demand, though my counter that the supply of would-be deans is far greater than the demand brought no response. All this discussion led to nothing, for we were operating from different premises: he from the notion that the faculty was to serve the administration, and I from the very opposite view.

The attitude of faculty members toward administration is often conditioned by the salary scale. From president to dean to department head to assistant professor the salaries may be in the ratio of 5 to 3 to 2 to 1. Thus the salaries of professors may be compressed in the range from five to ten thousand a year, while the president earns twenty-five thousand. One certain way to judge the quality of an institution is to measure the value administrators (who fix the salary scale) place on their own services, in relation to the faculty. How many professors are paid more than their department heads or deans?

In an institution where administrative position is too well paid in relation to scholarship, one can see ambitious faculty members, sometimes urged by their wives, scrambling for administrative favor. At one time I toyed with the notion of a parlor game in which the players would roll dice for points, and advance toward a goal called "Dean." A point score was to be devised for service-club membership, for speeches, for civic participation, for committee work and so on. Points were to be earned in proportion to time dissipated (that might otherwise have been spent in pursuit of learning). The conduct of a survey to determine the fraction of American institutions enrolling between four thousand and five thousand five hundred students that accept three hours of transfer credit, in research, toward the master's degree is the sort of useless activity that would have earned a good score. While the game was a joke, and we do not roll dice for points, a number of faculty members scramble avidly for them as though they had perceived that these were the basis of acquiring administrative positions, status and salary. Perhaps, under other circumstances, their time might have been spent more productively, in pursuit of the scholarship for which they were trained and in which they had demonstrated competence.

When I read the advice freely given to college presidents

by corporation executives, I am grateful for what we have, in spite of its shortcomings. The president of a major corporation which prides itself on progress once pontificated that colleges would be run more efficiently if the faculty were paid on a piecework basis, so much a head. The popular professor who lectured to droves of students would be well paid, while the professor who taught only few students would get what he deserved. In this admirable proposal it might be well to separate the role of the inspector from the pieceworker, in the university as in industry. Another distinguished executive announced with great flourish that colleges would be run more cheaply if class sizes were increased. This is again a profound and novel view. It is not at all clear to me that colleges would be better places if they were run by businessmen. Quite the contrary. I think it most unfortunate that college administrators sometimes pattern themselves after corporation executives, and that in the minds of the public and the boards of trustees the same confusion exists.

I do not know the solution to the problem of college administration, but I suspect that the business manager must be returned to his place, and that place is not one of establishing academic policy. I am convinced that administrators must be practical, that they must be capable of sacrificing principle to expediency. But I would be glad if the sacrifice were painful.

The great advantage in being a professor lies in the freedom a professor has to choose his research, and to do his teaching in his own way; that is, he has free choice after he has fulfilled a tremendous list of duties and obligations, and has satisfied some of the pressures upon him. In the budget a fraction of his time may be assigned to teaching, and this means classes which must be met; the balance is assigned to research and *other duties.* Those other duties? Consider the committee. This is another duty, a scheme for consuming endless amounts of time, without compensation, for losing touch with one's field completely. But then, points are garnered and local professional reputations are sometimes made in committee. Every college has a vast committee apparatus and even a corps of professional committeemen.

There is free choice in research, but funds are limited, and so the professor may be urged to undertake remunerative contracts off campus, for these will pay for the research, and provide a little overhead. In some universities a special system of commissions has been devised whereby a professor receives bonus pay for the contracts he garners. Under these circumstances there seems to be little attention paid to the quality of the work, whether it results in a weighty mimeographed report destined for burial in the contractor's files, or in a slim but meaningful publication. Nevertheless the award of a contract is greeted with a fanfare proportionate to the amount of the award, and the institution basks in the outside support received by its research program. In fact the program is not the program of the university but rather it is the program of the contractor, and the university may have taken on the aspect of a commercial research laboratory which has no program of its own but rather offers its facilities for hire. There are many occasions in which the program desired by the contractor and the research the professor would have done anyway are one and the same. But the word "contract" has a *quid pro quo* sound about it which tends to imply that the choice of research was tailored to suit those with the quid.

In an agricultural college such pressure may be exerted more subtly, for the college has a commitment to agricultural research as part of its mission. Thus I have learned to get a kick out of some of the work into which I was seduced by a good friend and neighbor nearly ten years ago. My work in the X-ray inspection of wheat led to other problems that were fun. I was able to devise a gadget for separating sound wheat from buggy wheat that I chose to call a "grain spectrometer," just to use a term from physics. More recently a new grain-hardness tester came from this activity. But the choice was not wholly free, for there was ready support for agricultural research.

Much has been said about the rewards of the superior teacher, and while teaching can be fun, the rewards have been somewhat overstated. The rewards are internal, and so is the knowledge that the teaching is superior. One hears about staying young by contact with young minds, but for me the best part of teaching is the sharpened perception of my subject that I get from repeated exposition. When my students look blank, I know that I have failed to understand a point or at least to develop it properly. Only in this sense is there benefit from contact with young minds. Teaching is sometimes a tremendous challenge in that the young minds need stimulating, and it may take the teacher's every resource to awaken them. It is a rare student that generates a new insight, even in research, if only for the reason that the student lacks the background to know whether his ideas are novel. From popular fiction everyone knows that behind the award and honor accorded a professor there is the brilliant but unrecognized graduate student from whom the idea was stolen. More likely the professor has worked for years to formulate a problem and to equip a laboratory. More often the professor reads the first draft of a student's thesis and thinks wearily that he is about to lose another weekend helping the student to straighten things out.

I would imagine that the freedom a professor has in his teaching varies with the field of his specialization. In physics there is a strong body of tradition which helps determine the content of a course. And there has never been any suggestion as to how I should teach my courses. As everywhere, the general physics course is one with considerable mortality. I am told that a motto hangs in the office of the president of one teachers' college which reads, "There are no F students, there is only F teaching." I wonder if it is not part of the problem of the physics teacher in college that there were no F students in the high schools. The courses students take in high school help to determine their choice of field in college. If the content of science and mathematics courses is at an unrealistically low level, and the grades are correspondingly high, it is easy to see that a student whose talents lie elsewhere might think himself suited for engineering. In defense of our own grading procedures, the results of a study (of physics grades in relation to the student's four-year average) showed that these were more tightly correlated than any other index available to the counseling center. As a result the student counselors now use the physics grade as one of the key pieces of information in helping the student make a choice of goals.

Why then does a professor remain on a faculty? The answer surely isn't salary. Professors are very conscious of the fact that they are underpaid in relation to their administrators and to their fee-earning counterparts, the lawyers, the dentists and the doctors. The professor's salary cannot buy the house, the books, the professional journals, the schools for his children that he must have, let alone the scale of living his television image boasts. He works in a world-wide competition in his research while his well-to-do professional counterpart rarely competes on even a county-wide level. I stay in this business because I like it. Those of us in a technical field are merchantable and feel that, if some crisis arises where we need more money, it is possible to find more gainful employment. But the case of the scientist or the engineer is somewhat special, and in many academic fields there is no place else to go. This is particularly true in the humanities where the professor is generally at the lower end of the university salary scale, and sometimes indecently so. Speeches on the value of scholarship lose their fullness when a professor in the humanities is valued at from $3500 to $5000 a year, in 1959, while a green Ph.D. in physics can start in industry at $9500.

With a built-in set of standards, a professor can enjoy his work. Without them, he spends his life jumping through other people's hoops. It is nice if your president knows you to be a first-rate teacher, but it is far more important that you know it and that you can derive occasional pleasure from the practice of this art. I chuckle when a dean tells me that it is just as easy to lecture to 150 as to 15, knowing that he has never done it and that he has never been around to wring me out after a lecture. It has been fun to pursue such diverse things as tornados and the Dirac monopole (a hypothetical particle of unit magnetic charge) without asking by your leave, as I could steal the time. Some of the things I've been interested in have worked out, and others have not. But compared to the years I spent in a government laboratory, my faculty years have been most productive. I have helped to process a couple or three thousand students in these ten years, and in the fourth of my time that the university has allocated to research, together with the night work they didn't pay for, I've managed (with collaborators) to get out a half-dozen papers in physics, a dozen or so in agricultural applications, a half-dozen popular pieces, and a textbook. In seven years in a government laboratory I wrote a great many reports, but all there is to show is one paper and two patents. And now I sign my own letters, rather than prepare them for the signature of the commanding officer. And there are no time clocks, though I put in longer hours.

I have been using administrators as whipping boys for the problems of the faculty and the university. But the blame does not lie with them. It lies with the public.

One day I was walking home across campus, and saw a student busily screwing light bulbs into a sign advertising the Engineer's Open House, an annual exposition staged by student engineers. I called to him and kidded, perhaps unfairly, that this was what he would probably be doing ten years hence, after he had his degree as an Electrical Engineer in hand.

"At least I won't teach school," he fired back.

About a year later I told this story at a banquet table of student engineers gathered to initiate new members into a professional fraternity, and was loudly and appreciatively applauded.

And then I asked the question that shut off the applause and closed the evening.

"Is this story funny because you don't think you're worth the hire of a good man?"

Kansas State University
of Agriculture and Applied Science

. . . Academic Freedom for What?

OTTO BUTZ

WHEN YOU get right down to it, it seems to me, we are all of us after the same thing in life. Our aim is to find fulfillment according to whatever values we happen to believe are most worth while. The differences in our actual behavior result, simply, from the fact that circumstances have given us different selves to fulfill and made available and attractive to us different values by which to be guided.

In my own life to date I have been conscious of five major directing values. Each of these is rooted in my background experiences and personality, and each has figured importantly in my choice of an academic career as well as in my subsequent reactions to it.

My most basic value—though not necessarily the one that most consistently guides me—has been my conviction that whatever success I achieve must be gained without injury to others and, where at all possible, must be justified by being used to help others in *their* quest for fulfillment. I acquired this conviction chiefly from my parents. From them I learned early that, as important as more abstract standards may be, the *most* important imperative in what would pretend to be truly Christian conduct is a sense of responsibility toward one's individual fellow man. So deeply was this injunction ingrained in me that the pangs of guilt and loss of self-respect I suffer when I violate it are the most painful feelings of which I am capable.

My second fundamental value has been a strong insistence upon the right to make up my own mind. At the most conscious level this has been a matter of philosophical conviction. As I see it, every man is inescapably responsible for his own actions and therefore under constant obligation to think them through to the limits of his own intelligence and conscience. Believing that this freedom and responsibility is one of our most precious human endowments, I have clung to it as jealously as possible. Whenever I have been compelled to abdicate it, I have felt frustrated and ashamed.

In a more subjective sense, on the other hand, my attachment to the right to do my own reflecting and choosing is a continuation of a response to which I found it necessary to resort while I was growing up. I was raised in an unassimilated German working-class family living in Canada. Since this was at the time immediately prior to and during World War II, I was obliged to live in what in effect were two largely separate and hostile worlds. To my German family belonged my emotional loyalties; in the surrounding Anglo-Saxon world were my schooling and prospective career. While my parents looked uneasily at my gradual emancipation from the family, the larger Canadian environment rejected me as an enemy alien and seemed to hold me personally responsible for every Nazi atrocity and every freighter that fell victim to a German submarine.

What to do? Repudiate my parents and my German background? (One well-meaning teacher even suggested I change my name to Oscar Butterfield!) Or retreat into the attitude of a submissive but resentful foreigner? The solution I only half-consciously stumbled upon was to defend my individuality against *both* of the worlds in which I was involved. I would continue to respect and remain devoted to my parents. And I would go at least halfway to meet the challenges of the world outside. But I would completely identify with neither; and I would let neither dictate my judgments and actions. I would conscientiously discharge my obligations. And I would make every effort to behave as a decent human being. But in return, I would exact from both of my worlds—and from whatever others I might encounter—the right to do my own thinking and choosing.

A third of my guiding norms has been a high valuation of any kind of excellence. In part this has been a matter of pride of workmanship. Seeing a job well done gives me a genuine feeling of exhilaration. It doesn't matter whether it be a musician's performance, a boxing match, a piece of craftsmanship, or a work of research. To earn this kind of satisfaction for myself, I am inclined to throw myself with almost reckless gusto into whatever challenge comes my way.

In origin, at least, my striving for excellence also has a more invidious dimension. This once again goes back to my experiences at school. The War and my German background caused me to be constantly taunted and made to feel inferior by many of my teachers and fellow students alike. I was excluded from every student office throughout my entire pre-college years. The climax came when at my high-school-graduation ceremony the principal refused to speak to me or even shake my hand. He limited himself to handing me the fistful of money prizes I had won and to explaining to my mother—some five years afterwards—that he hadn't been able to do otherwise since he himself had a German background and, consequently, had had to protect his job by showing no undue friendliness toward me.

Here, too, the alternatives seemed to be either to take it and feel defeated, or to fight back. Temperamentally disinclined to do the former, I was soon following a course that I subsequently found to be typical of disadvantaged minorities in general: I geared myself to outperform the members of the dominant group at whatever pursuits I could. As a result, I stood at the head of my class all the way through school and won every athletic and other contest for which I could possibly qualify. The reason, of course, was not superior ability but the seeming necessity of having to prove myself. It was only after I got to the University of Toronto and achieved greater acceptance and maturity that I realized what an empty and obnoxious motivation this was and gradually began to outgrow it.

Since I have been working for a living, I have acquired a much more purposeful incentive for wanting to excel. That has been the realization that the more competently I do my job, the less I am likely to be compelled to seek security and advancement by ingratiating myself socially or trimming my sails intellectually. Since this freedom is as important to me as it is, I tend to work much harder than would ordinarily be necessary.

Unfortunately, my variously motivated desire to excel constantly clashes with my already mentioned ideal of achieving fulfillment without deprivation to others. Obviously, if *I* compete successfully for a desirable academic position, the others who applied—however much they may want or need the job—will lose out. And the fifty students that *my* extra efforts gain for a course of lectures that *I* am giving, are a loss and a possible damage to the prospects of fulfillment of one or more *other* professors. In order to excel and maximize my independence without being involved in this moral dilemma, I find myself constantly searching for possibilities of satisfying achievement *outside* of the regular organizational frameworks. What I seem in effect to be striving for is some kind of role in which, ideally, I can be myself and get mine, with a minimum of inhibition to others in being themselves and getting theirs.

My fourth major directing value is a very high esteem for intellectual understanding. This again is a matter of conviction as well as of background experiences. While I by no means despise the pleasures of the senses, I derive my richest and most sustained satisfactions from using my mind and knowing. I believe that it is in man's possession of this faculty that he stands out most markedly from the other animals. I therefore also hold that it is in his greatest possible use of this faculty that he achieves his highest realization as a human being.

But I do not merely revere knowledge for the human ennoblement it represents. Ever since my schooldays I have felt a deep personal need for it to help me make sense out of and orient myself to my environment. First my isolated position as a foreigner, and later my determination to defend my individuality made it impossible for me ever to take my environment for granted. I have found it necessary to think through almost every relationship and situation in which I have been involved. Even in high school I was an avid reader of whatever books on philosophy, history and psychology the small school library permitted me to get my hands on. It was not that anyone encouraged me to do so. I simply needed to know who I was and why, and where I and everyone else seemed to be going and why.

Because of this conception and role of knowledge in my life, my pursuit of it is primarily neither a matter of doing something to enhance my prestige as a scholar nor of earning money to keep up with this or that status. In a sense, I see life as a voyage of discovery—of myself, of other people, and of the forces in and around us. The more I understand, the more fully I live. I majored in political science because I wanted to know the nature of international relations and of the phenomenon of Nazism. Since then my interests have broadened into a quest for an understanding of the condition and prospects of contemporary civilization as a whole. And always—whatever subject matter I select for special study—my basic purpose is the same: to discover and savor life's complexities and to try to gain a glimpse into what it all adds up to.

My fifth and final guiding value is a strong belief that everyone should in some constructive way contribute to the operation of society as a whole. I do not find it enough that a man merely live without damaging others or, even, that he limit himself to helping others as individuals. Somehow, I feel, one should also be participating in some kind of more collectively directed role. One always *is,* of course—whether it be as a farmer, a craftsman, a businessman, or anything else. Yet in my case I want to *know* how what I am doing fits into the larger scheme of things. Being as independent and private in my motivations as I am, I need at least a clearly perceivable intellectual tie-in with society's larger processes and problems.

This need, however, is in constant potential conflict with my militant individuality which is at the root of it. For while

I insist on the one hand that the individual is essentially his own justification, I believe equally firmly that he should vindicate his existence through some kind of definable service to society as a whole.

Unfortunately, I see no final solution to this dilemma—save to avoid getting into the kind of situation in which one would actually have to *choose* between one's individual and collective rationale. I suspect that if I *were* confronted with such a choice I would take the same course that Pasternak adopted for his Dr. Zhivago. That is, I would wish society well and go my own way, however difficult it might be. Yet I would do so with more pangs of conscience than Dr. Zhivago appears to have suffered. For the fact, for example, that Pasternak's hero had children by three different wives—all of whom it fell to others who *were* identified with the system to raise and pay for—did not seem to bother him in the least. I am afraid that my individuality is not that morally self-sufficient. I would at least make every effort to pay the price of my own way of life and actions. And I would constantly feel the need to justify myself and search for some way, however modest, in which I *might* again contribute to the function of the whole.

For the past five years I have been attempting to find fulfillment according to the above values in the role of a college professor. In the course of that experience I have felt the satisfaction of delivering a well-prepared and well-received lecture; have known the exciting give and take of searching philosophical bull sessions; have had the delightful sense of usefulness in helping bright students with their intellectual as well as personal growing pains; have enjoyed the thrill of what seemed to me significant research; and have made a living—albeit not an overly fat one.

As a result of a combination of top graduate-school grades from Princeton, an alive wit and appearance, and luck, I was able to land jobs at two first-rate schools—first Swarthmore and then Princeton—and to manage, even, to skip the instructor step in the ladder and start right in as an assistant professor. And because, I suspect, I am genuinely interested in people and ideas and have not acquired too many of the mannerisms of the current American version of the *Herr Professor,* I have gone over well with students. Indeed, until I became a *bête noire* because I defied Princeton University's stern warning not to publish what seemed to me a rather innocent but thought-provoking collection of autobiographical essays by Princeton seniors (*The Unsilent Generation*), mine could have passed for a rather model academic success story. An associate professorship—and the lifetime tenure that goes with it—seemed just around the corner. As one of my superiors put it—in urging me to be what he considered sensible and to throw the student essays in question into an incinerator —I appeared to have it "made."

But I had been becoming increasingly disenchanted with the academic life for several years. My disappointments were of two kinds. Least serious, though most annoying, were what I found to be academia's shortcomings from a human point of view. Somehow, I had had the impression that the pursuit and teaching of higher learning were a rather dignified business. To my dismay, the pettiness, backbiting and organizational timidity that I encountered (and at times had no alternative but to participate in to defend myself) turned out to be worse than in any other type of job I had ever held before. As a result, at least most of the younger men—including myself—often came to worry more about whether they had said "the wrong thing" at a departmental meeting, or whether this or that senior professor or his wife liked them, than about the actual work to be done.

In part, I admit, these human disappointments have been due to my own unrealistic expectations. If material success and social approval are the chief conscious aspirations of Americans in general, it is little wonder that the same weakness of what Riesman has called "inner direction" prevails among American professors. At best, moreover, human nature being what it is, a certain amount of such antics is probably inevitable and must simply be put up with.

The more extreme "rat race" aspects of the academic life, however, I believe to be a symptom of a much more immediate and specific shortcoming from which American higher learning is today suffering. That, it seems to me from my own observations and my current reading, is its deep and demoralizing uncertainty as to what it is really doing and how it really fits into contemporary culture as a whole. For though American professors are eloquent as ever in their claims to academic freedom, they show little awareness of the larger opportunities and responsibilities that that freedom may, in our present type of society, have come to entail. Instead, for example, of finding inspiration in such a vital task as contributing to the nation's cultural and political leadership, they are increasingly bogging down in professional particularism, erudition and ritual.

Striking evidence of this apparent crisis of academic purpose is revealed in two widely publicized recent novels by and about American professors, Carlos Baker's *A Friend in Power,* and Stringfellow Barr's *Purely Academic.* Both of these books are the work of thoroughly knowledgeable academic insiders. And both are centrally concerned with a college professor's dilemma whether to stick to his calling as a scholar and teacher or to forsake it for some more lucrative and prestigeful career. Yet in neither, significantly, does the author face up to what in each is the key dramatic and philosophical issue: what it really *means* to be an academic, that is, why one would be attached to the activities academia represents and what one would lose in abandoning them.

In *A Friend in Power,* for example, repeated mention is made of the hero's determination to complete a major manuscript on Voltaire. But why Voltaire? Why any kind of research and writing at all? Is its purpose merely to lend formal reaffirmation to the hero's professional standing as a scholar? If so, are we to assume that scholars constitute a world entirely unto themselves? Do they not also require some larger rationale through a meaningful relationship to society as a whole? Unfortunately, the author of *A Friend in Power* nowhere even raises these fundamental questions.

Similarly with Professor Baker's characterization of college teaching. Why teach? To combat ignorance, we are informed: "Ignorance, he [the hero] thought. The great foe of us all—and the collaborating friend. All year long we will fight it, in all the forms it takes. This is what we are about: this is our job, our private war. . . ."

But what kind of ignorance are we fighting? With what kind of enlightenment? And what is the enlightenment to accomplish for society and mankind at large? Again, Professor Baker either cannot say or does not think it important to say.

No more thoroughly thought through is the role of higher learning as depicted in Stringfellow Barr's *Purely*

Academic. The professor-hero in this case becomes progressively disillusioned with the life of scholar and teacher and takes refuge in the more genteel existence of a foundation executive. Why? Because, as he complains, "nothing whatever" is happening at his Midwestern college. "At least nothing relevant to a liberal education. . . . There's no common purpose. The trustees want to prevent subversion and stay solvent. The President . . . wants to get publicity. . . . The department heads want to raid each other for students. . . . The professors want to publish, get promoted, get famous, and meanwhile stave off their creditors."

When Barr's hero, speaking to his future sponsor in the foundation, admits that the situation may be less sterile elsewhere, the latter quickly disabuses him: "Don't be silly. . . . What you've just described is a coast-to-coast operation. . . . The thing to do is not to take it too seriously. . . . I detect a certain intellectual honesty in you. I like it. But you mustn't let it confuse you. If you do, you'll never get ahead."

But if, in Professor Barr's view, "nothing relevant to a liberal education" is happening, the question is posed as to *what should or could be happening?* Yet the author of *Purely Academic* shows himself no more prepared to venture an answer to this fundamental question than is Professor Baker in his *A Friend in Power.*

That this professional myopia is bound to be reflected in academia's internal organization and performance goes without saying. Its effect upon academic recruitment, for example, appears clearly from Theodore Caplow's and Reece J. McGee's *The Academic Marketplace.* For what this investigation of the academic hiring process conclusively shows is "that the chief criteria used in making appointments are prestige and compatibility." Academic prestige, moreover, is found to be based "on scholarly achievement and not on teaching ability." And scholarly achievement, finally, turns out to be "judged by a survey of opinion rather than a survey of published works: the printed material gathered or submitted for that judgment is looked at but not read."

But given academia's prevailing professional self-centeredness, what type of scholarly writings are likely to be accorded greatest prestige? And what type of professor is likely to be found most compatible? Obviously, and as Caplow and McGee have in fact shown, those who conform to the established academic expectations are strongly favored; and those who challenge them tend to be found controversial and excluded. The end result, of course, is not only to perpetuate academia's life unto itself but constantly to reinforce it.

The consequence of these narrowly professional expectations for the scope of academic research and writing are well known: on the one hand a tense insistence on highly specialized description and abstract methodology; and on the other an equally assiduous discouragement of anything that might smack of value judgment and general interpretation. As Professor V. O. Key has noted about current writing in political science, for example, "Our journals are still in large measure filled with treatments of particular events, institutions, practices. Often these are well done . . . yet they add absolutely nothing by way of general idea." And as another distinguished American scholar, Abraham Kaplan, felt moved to apologize in undertaking an interpretive essay on such a vital subject as "American Ethics and Public Policy," "There is an academic sin which cannot be forgiven, the sin against specialization. Every writer must be an expert, and every expert must write only on his own specialty—unless, to be sure, there has been ritual expiation by communion in an interdisciplinary project. . . . But setting out alone, as I am, I approach the reader burdened with a presumption of guilt."

Nor does this inhibiting conception of the role of academia fail to leave its effects upon college teaching. One hears a great deal about the decline in recent years in the American professor's lecture-room impact. And most often this is ascribed to the alleged apathy and lack of seriousness of today's students. Yet there is considerable evidence that the chief fault, rather, may lie with the failure of too many American professors to make their materials meaningful enough in broader than merely professional academic terms.

In the collection of student essays alluded to above, for example, the student-authors' associations with their professors appeared to have left little memorable effect upon them. The book's academic reviewers were quick to see in this yet another indication of today's students' lack of reverence for the world of higher learning. Yet what these reviewers almost uniformly failed to note was the telling nature of the few comments that the students contributing to the book *did,* in fact, devote to the subject of their professors.

One young man, for instance—a highest honors student and himself headed for an academic career—bluntly complained that "United States universities, while they offer magnificent opportunities for learning, seem to me to fall short in respect to their faculties. There are more scholars than teachers. . . . Most professors accept a position at a university in order to have a chance to study or to provide for their families. . . . They fail to grasp the essence of teaching and by so doing fail to arouse the minds of their pupils as effectively as they could."

Another of these college seniors, also a top student in his class, explained that the reason he chose to major in his university's history department was that as a freshman he had taken a course with a truly inspiring teacher, "an ancient professor with a prominent hearing aid and atrocious taste in clothes. He lectured too early in the morning. . . . The reading assignments were three times as long as those in other courses. Yet approximately one quarter of the student body elected his course. He was magnificent. Apparently one of the last of the individualist professors, he lectured on twentieth-century war and revolution. I hope he gave the others, as he gave me, a faith in the power of the individual to advance human society in triumph over apparently insuperable odds." Unfortunately, this student regretfully adds, "I was disappointed, for the old gentleman in question retired that same year. Though there were historians on the faculty who had studied under him, none had assimilated his philosophy as I understood it. Most of them are pedantic, crushing bores, afraid of their own ideas and ashamed of their own individuality."

Though these are only the opinions of anonymous undergraduates, they may well point to an important truth. For indications abound that today's students—perhaps much more strongly than the youth of a generation or two ago—in fact *do* feel a deep need for the larger meaning and orientation that higher learning can provide. If these young people often appear intellectually apathetic, this may be less a matter of indifference to higher learning as such than of disillusionment at their professors' failure to make the most of its full potentialities.

As we know from the fate that befell higher learning in Nazi Germany, the lack of a positive enough sense of larger academic responsibility may, under certain circumstances, result in the most dangerous consequences even for academic freedom itself. The only case of such circumstances in recent American experience has, of course, been the pressures exerted upon higher learning during the McCarthy period. Yet the lesson demonstrated is nonetheless ominous. For as appears from Paul F. Lazarsfeld's and Wagner Thielens Jr.'s study, *The Academic Mind,* the predominant response of American professors to the McCarthy situation was anything but heroic. It was, indeed, largely one of resigned self-pity and submissiveness.

What customarily gives men the will resolutely to fight back against intimidation is the conviction that they themselves and what they represent are simply too unique and important to be allowed to be violated. Yet—to judge by the twenty-four hundred sample interviews reported on in *The Academic Mind*—it was precisely this kind of conviction that American professors did not clearly and strongly enough possess. For, as Lionel Trilling has commented in regard to the Lazarsfeld and Thielens findings, "At no point do any of the responses suggest that the pressures in this instance had been exerted upon a very special group, upon scholars, upon men of mind. Indeed, nothing is more striking than the teachers' inability to think of themselves as special in any way—as special because they are superior, as special because they have a certain relation to ideas, as special because they are committed to certain ideas."

To remedy this crisis of American academic purpose, current efforts merely to improve the organization and financing of higher learning seem to me far from enough. What would appear to be required is nothing less than a fundamental re-relating of the role of academia to society's life as a whole, and particularly to its need for leadership.

Cultural and political direction in times past could be counted upon either from the rule of a traditional aristocracy or through the initiative of various movements of popular discontent and reform. In neither case was there any extensive direct dependence on organized higher learning. It was therefore not at all unreasonable for the inhabitants of academia to pursue their work almost exclusively for its own sake and for whatever satisfactions they themselves might derive from it. Since the operation of society as a whole required nothing immediate from them, they for their part needed only to insist upon their academic freedom, their right to be left alone and uninvolved.

In a liberal democracy like the present-day United States, the persistence of such a limited and passive role for academia is a dangerous anachronism. For higher learning has become an integral part of a type of society whose direction *cannot* any longer be taken for granted. There *are* no more traditional aristocracies or popular movements of discontent and reform to tell us where we are going and how we should get there. Cultural and political leadership in our contemporary social order must be consciously and constantly worked at.

And for the performance of this crucial task of *thinking and teaching for leadership* no one is as well prepared and strategically placed as are our academics. Indeed, who else in this busy, organizationally fragmented society retains the necessary detachment, knowledge and opportunity? Who else, if not our professors, is sufficiently steeped in our civilization's heritage to interpret its meaning for the issues of our here and now? And when, if not during their years at college, are our leaders and citizens of tomorrow to be imbued with the sense of continuity and purpose that their part in the unfolding of the nation's potentialities will demand?

From an aristocratic luxury for the cultural satisfaction of a few, academic freedom has been transformed by events into a vital instrument for the welfare and fulfillment of the many. And in being so transformed, it has also become a freedom that must be constantly exercised and earned. It will remain important to those who enjoy it and will be supported by society as a whole *only to the extent that it is employed to the full measure of its new opportunities and responsibilities.*

This, it seems to me, is the twentieth-century challenge to which our academics must at last rise. In meeting it they could gain a badly needed new sense of larger function with which to overcome the currently prevalent and demoralizing feeling of being little more than talking textbooks. They could acquire a new sense of essentials to inspire them to engage in sustained and truly reflective scholarship rather than, as happens all too often now, frittering away their time and brains in mere promotion-minded publishing-or-perishing. And they could win a measure of popular appreciation which the profession of higher learning has never before enjoyed. For what would be recognized to be at stake would be not merely the happiness of a group of morally isolated and culturally aloof experts but, in a real sense, the vitality and welfare of the whole society.

Perhaps, I sometimes reproach myself, my critical reactions to contemporary American academia are much ado about nothing. Perhaps all is for the best and I am only rationalizing from my own personality and my own particular values. But I do not think so. It seems clear to me that now, when the age-old utopia of freedom from want and exploitation is in process of being realized, we must look harder than ever at what we are becoming and where we could or should be going. It is possible, of course, that we have reached a new and secularized version of the Middle Ages in which everyone can happily find and adjust to his place, in which the whole can be assumed to operate automatically, and in which the inspiration and criticism of morally involved yet organizationally detached intellectuals is no longer needed.

Yet I, at least, cannot convince myself that this is the case. And on the assumption that it is not I shall continue to base my teaching, research and writing—whether I am on the payroll of a first-rate or a third-rate university, whether what I produce is considered political science in the narrow sense or published under some other rubric, and whether I ever become wealthy and prestigeful or not. I naturally hope that I *will* in the end harvest my share of material and social rewards. But even if I should not, I will at least enjoy being myself and acting according to my own views and convictions. And, as an old Jewish friend of mine used to say: "In America, anyway, nobody starves."

Princeton University

... *The Acceptance of Obscurity*

JAY A. YOUNG

MY FATHER, to whom I owe a great deal, once told me that justification is as necessary for sanity as breathing is necessary for physical well-being. By that he meant, I think, that somehow every individual must satisfy himself that his every action and thought is reasonable, at least to himself. My own observations have not led me to a different conclusion. Yet, it is not easy to find this reasonableness in my own choice for a life's work. It is easy to know why in the little things, but it is difficult to know why in the things that count the most. Why did I marry that particular girl that I did marry? Why did I choose to be a college professor? Why did I choose to teach chemistry?

Looking back, I think my father was something of a cynic. He meant, when he said that justification was necessary, that often our justification is merely a subjective reason conditioned by our attitude, and far from the real, true reason. I suspect that those who disagree with the premises from which I shall draw my own reasons will find sufficient evidence to indicate that in my case, at least, my reasons are not objective, that they have been formulated after the choice was made and are therefore not the real reasons that caused me to choose what I have chosen.

I would not deny this myself. I have kept no diary. I do not know why it was, before I chose to become a professor, that I decided to become one. I do know, now, why I am glad I did so choose. Perhaps this is not too uncommon. Perhaps only a few would be able to say that the reasons they had for choosing a life's work are the same reasons they now hold for continuing in their choice. In my own case, I suspect that the reasons, now forgotten, that caused me to choose my vocation were superficial. Or, to be more honest about it, it is only now, with maturity, that I have found good reasons for the fortuitous choice that was made, then, in the foolishness of youth.

Before presenting these reasons, however, it may be helpful to describe a few indicative experiences from my earlier years. Perhaps these experiences had more to do with the matter than I suspect. It is difficult to put early memories in chronological order, but one of my earliest is of a visit with the principal of our parish parochial school. I was five at the time and I recall reading for Sister from a second-grade primer. Apparently I passed the examination.

My father had taught high-school chemistry and physics before I was born and had later become a chiropractor. Shortly before I reached the age of two he determined to perform an experiment that, as far as I can tell, has turned out successfully. He had observed that a child of eighteen months could identify toy animals by name. He reasoned that it should be possible, therefore, for a young child to recognize the letters of the alphabet. And, just possibly, to be able to put these letters together and recognize words. The phonetic method for teaching reading was just then (this was in 1922) becoming well known, and by use of this method I was taught to read. Four years were required. I entered the third grade at the age of six and passed.

In the next summer I was taught the intricacies of long division and other fourth-grade topics. My father's niece lived with us at the time. She was then teaching the fourth grade in one of the schools in the public-school system. Patient girl that she was, she convinced me, against my own opinion, that the technique of long division was not quite the same as the technique used when the divisor had only one digit. I can still remember the violence with which I resisted the introduction of this new concept. My cousin's pedagogical problems were greater than is ordinarily the case; by the time of that summer, she had been living at our home, as a sister to me, for two or three years. A boy of six never accepts any instruction from an older sister, but I am glad now that her solicitude was superior to my bullheadedness. I not only learned long division, but I also learned that teaching is a joyful thing. To patiently overlook the resistance of a pupil requires an inner sense of peace that arises from the intellectual satisfaction inherent in the act of teaching. From that summer's tutoring, I know now, I began to understand this important principle.

I entered the fifth grade that fall and continued to progress in a proper manner. At that time, however, the teaching in our parochial school had become less than good. Halfway through the sixth grade my father transferred me to the public-school system. I did not return to a Catholic school until 1940, when I began work for the doctorate degree at Notre Dame.

There had been some criticism of my father because he placed me ahead of my age group in school. I was aware of this criticism, but I am still doubtful of its validity. My classmates were always courteous, solicitous because of my smaller size; no one ever, except for very rare instances that have been all but forgotten, bullied me or took advantage of the three years' difference in age. My grades were average or slightly above. As a teacher now, I can understand how my own teachers might have tended to impute more ability to me than I possessed.

Outside of school I played with companions of my own age. In school my friends were my classmates. This disparity in ages, the existence of two sets of friends, did not seem untoward to me. There were no "social" difficulties of which I was ever aware. I have not been driven into academics because of an early social prejudice against my bookishness.

It is true that because of my smaller size, I was not able to participate effectively in athletic activities at school. My classmates prudently assigned me to left field in playground baseball games, but they did let me play even though all knew that a ball hit to my area was a sure home run. Eventually more prudence was exercised as my lack of proficiency became clearly evident; I recall some strong demands to umpire the games instead of gentle requests that I play even as a fielder. Because I played poorly, I had found little pleasure as a chosen member of a team and I did enjoy the authority of the umpire, so the change was a happy one. Perhaps I also learned some of the rudiments of the techniques I now use as a teacher. These two activities are not dissimilar.

In another way, perhaps with a greater permanent effect, my father influenced my character and effected my teaching. In memory, this other influence seems to run as a theme, coloring all the incidental events that I can now recall. As the eldest of three children I had many chores ranging from simple housekeeping duties to errand-running and care of the average-sized grounds around our home. I spent much more time on such tasks than my friends did. Probably I was required to do only slightly more than the average child, for this was my father's way, but I worked slowly and half-heartedly. It was his custom to inspect each completed task and, as a matter of policy, to be dissatisfied with any first efforts. No doubt anyone, except my mother, would have been displeased with my work. I carried out many assigned tasks several times before my father indicated his acceptance. This was so strongly emphasized that even to this day I find it unsettling when other duties demand that I turn away from a semi-completed task that I think has not yet been done to the best of my ability.

Thus, there is usually too little time available in my courses to fully discuss all of the important topics. There is never sufficient time to help the poorer students understand many of the topics. Although I have sought for a satisfactory solution without success, I have been able to identify the items that give students the most difficulty and to clarify these obscurities to some extent.

As I grew older my father became interested, as an intellectual avocation, in psychology. Characteristically, after thorough and well-planned study, he devised his own notions and applied them in a practical manner. Much of his thought on these matters I now recognize as worth while, although I cannot and did not agree with all of his ideas. Insofar as I can determine, however, he attempted to inculcate in me only his less radical notions. During my middle and late teens, his emphasis was upon the absolute necessity to learn the other person's point of view. He called this "projection," and this word epitomizes his over-all views. He studied this notion, the validity and utility of a conscious effort to know another's views as though they were one's own, in all kinds of hypothetical circumstances. He then made sure that I was cognizant of the inter-person relationships arising in these hypothetical situations and helped me to understand how to determine the correct action in such a situation. I have since learned that the hypothetical circumstances were not so imaginary after all, and have been able to profit from his solicitous interest in many ways.

Consider the college freshman who is unsuited for the vocational choice made for him by his parents (a frequent problem, even today), but who attempts as best he can to carry out their wishes. Such a young man will not often meet the academic requirements of the prescribed curriculum. Caught between two strongly felt forces—his parents' wishes and his own lack of ability—such a student is often discouraged. I can help this student only to the degree that I can understand his feelings and those of his parents. The conflict must be resolved or at least allayed if such a student is to do well in any course of study.

Valuable though they were, my father's ideas on "projection" were tinged with a materialism that was not wholly acceptable to me. But I have found that his ideas, coupled with my own certainty of the existence of a personal, rational soul—equipped with a will, with an intellect, with appetites that can (and some that cannot) be mentioned in print, and with other attributes—have enabled me to get along successfully with the many different kinds of individuals that I meet as a teacher.

In retrospect it is clear that my early environment was well suited to the training of a teacher. Our bookshelves were well stocked. I remember best the books from my father's teaching days. There must have been more than thirty high-school chemistry and physics texts and I suspect that I read every one at least in part. I used them as references—extracting information for the construction of my own electromagnets, motors, telephones, electrostatic voltage machines and similar devices. Most of these did not function. I had a chemistry set, too, but I never did finish all of the experiments in the instruction manual. Either the physics books were more interesting to me at the time, or they were better written. I can still see some of the pages of those physics books, but of the chemistry texts, I can recall only the color of the covers, splotched with chemical stains.

There were other books available. I recall one on the highest shelf, titled *Madame X,* that I never did read (no doubt a worth-while abstention). *Pilgrim's Progress* was on a lower shelf. I found it dull, but I read every word. I remember *The Deserted Village* with pleasure, and there were other works of Goldsmith though I forget their names. I remember *Heidi* with distaste. I found *Alice in Wonderland* only mildly interesting; I still doubt that it is a child's book. *Grimm's Fairy Tales* were delightful. Rumpelstiltskin is still an evocative word for me. There were two or three sets of multi-volumed anthologies, filled with many things. Interesting stories, some well known to everyone, some not. They also contained suggestions for things to make. The directions I found in one such set of books described the construction of a crystal radio set, but included no reference to a source of power. I corrected this obvious omission and survived, wiser but sadder. It was not until I reached high school that I was ever able to construct a working crystal set. These anthologies also contained interesting anecdotes about exploration, interesting facets of natural history, and rules for games. Although I did participate in some active forms of play, most of my time was spent in reading or in playing with the half-technical toys of my own construction. (In general I tried to determine why they were inoperative.) I was able to convince my friends of the pleasures of this kind of play sufficiently so that there were frequent occasions for mutual give and take. When I learned the meaning of the word, I suspected that I was introverted, but I doubt that this was the case. If it was, the syndrome has long since disappeared.

Lindbergh made his solo flight when I was six. I recall my own resolution to one day become equally famous by means of an equally adventurous achievement. This ambition changed as I became more interested in the science books available to me. I still wanted to earn the acclaim but for a different accomplishment. It would be better to be honored as another Einstein. In the longer view that I am now able to take, it is clear that I was beginning to learn the fascination of the questions "How?" and "Why?" Before a man can become a chemist, he must learn to respect these words; to become a teacher of chemistry a man must learn to treasure them. Today, because I know that I am well suited to be a teacher, the joy in imparting this treasure has eclipsed my earlier desire for the shallower rewards of fame.

My first interest in chemistry probably came from my high-school course. Had physics been offered before chemistry, I would probably have chosen physics. The same teacher taught both subjects and he taught them well. I cannot say how well he taught the elementary principles and facts of the subjects, for I had learned these things before, from my own reading, but he made it very clear, to everyone, that chemistry was interesting. Mr. Plasterer liked soap bubbles.

A man who can be deeply enough interested in soap bubbles to entertain audiences with them for two or three hours, as he did, and still does, can infect the most recalcitrant pupil. I do not think I was recalcitrant; I was infected; I still am; I do know that from then on, I determined to be a chemist; perhaps I even then also became infected with the joys of teaching.

During these years I attended Mass regularly every Sunday because I was obedient to my parents' wishes. Under duress, during Lent, I occasionally made the Stations of the Cross. But Sunday Mass to me then seemed enough and I avoided the extra requirements as much as possible, with frequent success. Despite my obstinacy, the influence of the religious practices of these early years did gently prepare me to change my aims, to achieve a better ambition. I first became conscious of the tawdriness of my earlier ambitions when I attended Notre Dame as a graduate student. I learned that academic excellence is important, and that it is expedient to seek this excellence. But I also learned that man is subject to his Creator and that it is, therefore, wise to satisfy His demands. I began to understand that neither the expediency of achieving academic excellence nor the prudence of virtue include the acclaim of other men as a necessary or desirable achievement.

The insistence on academic excellence was overt; the suggestion that the practice of virtue is wise was subtle. In the early 1940's at Notre Dame little attention was paid to the religious needs of the graduate students. For the undergraduates it was a different matter. In particular, a weekly mimeographed sheet on the practical applications of the Catholic faith was distributed to the undergraduates. By intent or by accident, I received these weekly bulletins. They altered my life. At that time, the priest who prepared the bulletins was interested in increasing the number of daily communicants. He discussed this theme from many viewpoints and he convinced me, as well as many others. I began to receive Holy Communion daily, when possible, and have not stopped yet. I believe that the graces received as a result of this habit have been responsible for whatever good there is now in me. Purely as a practical matter, I would not wish to lose this habit. To me, religious matters must be viewed practically. In this life, religion is a tool, not an end.

To avoid the accusation of heresy, however, an explanation is needed. Prudent selfishness is a virtue. I must think of myself first. I serve my own interests best when I understand myself to be a creature, subservient to the omnipotent Triune Creator. To the degree that I practice, in act and in thought, the conclusions that can be drawn from this premise, I act wisely. Viewed in this light, the Catholic religion is an ordered arrangement, fully logical, of precepts, of facts, and of recommendations drawn from these facts. From these I can determine the prudence or the foolishness of any act or thought. I am bound in conscience to use this information to determine the prudence of every act, before it is performed. I am bound in conscience to examine any thought I may think. These considerations are more important than any others because they pertain to eternity. Other laudible practices, important though they may be, are concerned only with the present life as their direct object. It would be foolish to trade an infinite inheritance for the brass of fame.

Since my task is to teach chemistry, it is clear that I must teach this subject to the best of my ability. If I have a student who seems naturally adapted to a study of this subject, I must make sure that this ability is developed further. If I have a less fortunate student, I must at least make sure that he learns as much chemistry as he can and that he also learns how this science is intimately integrated with those studies in which he is proficient. By example, surely, and perhaps occasionally by counsel, I can help a student to learn that he must meet two requirements—excellence in his chosen field and subservience to the Creator's demands. But I must make it clear that to be excellent in a chosen field is an act of subservience. Few men are hermits; ordinarily, to fail to serve other men to an excellent degree is to fail to serve Him who made those fellow men.

By the middle of 1941 I had already earned a master's degree at Oberlin College and had had an additional year of graduate study in chemistry at Notre Dame. Perhaps my immaturity is in evidence here, but when I was offered an unsolicited position as Chief Chemist (I was the only chemist to be employed) at a brake-lining manufacturing plant in Huntington, Indiana, my home town, I accepted. I was tired of school and wanted to enjoy the presumed benefits of a regular salary. Since most of my students become industrial chemists, either immediately or after earning a graduate degree, this experience in nonacademic chemistry is profitable. Different industries vary widely in their particular practices and policies, but over-all there is a distinct similarity. It is good to be able to know of the kinds of problems my students will face when they become practicing chemists. Occasions often arise in teaching when this information can be imparted to them for their ultimate benefit.

The work with brake linings was interesting, particularly the vocabulary. The erratic action of automobile brakes in the early morning, due to the deposition of dew on the brake linings, is known as "morning sickness." This has been my only experience with this phenomenon. (Blessed with twelve children thus far, Mrs. Young has not suffered from this unpleasant malady.)

The authority was enjoyable. To be a student requires a certain humility. If this humility is not already present, it is imposed by the teacher, for one who learns must understand that he is a learner. The transition from forcefully humbled student to authoritative Chief Chemist was violent but not at all unpleasant. Under my direction laboratory technicians prepared all kinds of mixtures, from powdered coal and finely ground nut hulls to 1, 2-dihydroxyanthraquinone and methylphenyldiimide with asbestos and other ingredients. These mixtures were then formed into experimental brake linings and tested by adventurous men in test cars. We made a very good experimental lining one day, so good that it would stop a car very quickly. This particular lining could not be made in a uniform manner, although we did not know this until later. One piece of this experimental lining had more, or less, drag than another supposedly similar piece. This lining was installed on a test car and when the brakes were applied to the rapidly moving car, it spun around on a dry pavement. The chastened driver informed me that he thought this method of stopping a car impractical. Test drivers are inclined to be philosophical as well as adventurous, so we remained good friends. Shortly thereafter, in early 1942, our test drivers resumed a normal existence. Brake-lining chemists were not readily exempt from the draft.

I became a civilian employee with the War Department, eventually becoming a specialist, for what it is worth, in military pyrotechnics. By 1944 it became necessary to join the Navy to avoid the Army, a choice I have never regretted.

Late in the summer of 1944 I completed the naval indoctrination course and confidently expected orders, as a very unwilling ensign, to the amphibious forces. It was said that ensigns led the troops ashore, armed with a .45 and marked for the enemy by a billed cap. Most ensigns, it was said, never had need to reload their .45 more than once. As it happened, I never learned the truth or the falsity of these statements, but, as a Catholic, if I was to die, I had better make plans.

That year, at the age of twenty-three, I was aware of the finality of death and of the serious consequences of death in the state of mortal sin. By this time, for reasons that still puzzle me, I had read, even studied, a series of elementary textbooks which dealt with logic, ontology, ethics, and all the rest, from a Catholic viewpoint. I knew, though it was hard to admit it even to myself, what would happen to me if I died unrepentant. Here was a clear alternative: either sincerely renounce the mortal errors of the past and resolve to at least try to avoid such error in the future or take the consequences. The Catholic chaplain heard my confession.

Sincere repentance is a serious matter. To ask for forgiveness implies sorrow for the infraction. And to have sorrow requires a resolution to avoid the infraction in the future. I had made this resolution easily; it would be necessary to keep it for only a few months more. I have been stuck with it ever since. In its wisdom the Navy assigned me to a desk-laboratory job, quite safe from bullets, but unprotected from more subtle terrors, from temptations to err again.

From this time on I began to learn a difficult lesson. Only conformity to the will of God brings peace of mind. I have not yet learned this perfectly. We all seek pleasure, or happiness, or joy, but when attained, these satisfactions are evanescent. It is discouraging to see them disappear; there must be some achievable condition that will bring permanent satisfaction.

To me it is reasonable to believe that I can achieve a permanent peace of mind only by conforming to God's will, since it was He who put this desire for satisfaction in me in the first place. This has been forced upon me by the logic of the matter. I do not like to give in; it is easier to be proud, but pride pays with the vaporous coin of pleasure. I prefer a more stable coin. Somehow, in trying to accept God's will, I have become a teacher. I am pleased with the choice.

My experiences in industry and in the government had, by the end of the war, convinced me that I would be happier in another kind of work. Looking back, my dissatisfaction was not due to the nature of the work, or to the associates with whom I worked. It was rather due to my own petulance, which I saw as a reflection, having imputed the cause of my dissatisfaction to the conditions and to my associates. With the mellowness that has come with mature youth (at thirty-eight I am still ten years or more from middle age and will continue to be at least this far from the beginning of senescence for some time to come), I am sure that I could have been as happy in any work related to chemistry as I have now found myself to be in teaching. I am sure that I am quite satisfied as a teacher, but happiness does not depend upon externals. I was unaware of this then.

It was, however, quite clear that if I aspired to excellence, and especially if I wished to receive the recognition of my peers for that excellence, a doctorate degree was essential.

With the help of the G.I. Bill, with the consideration of my teachers (some of whom did not seem to be considerate at all at the time) and by dogged, persistent effort, encouraged by my wife, solicitous for the future welfare of my family, I earned a doctorate degree in chemistry from the University of Notre Dame.

College instructors in chemistry were scarce then, even more scarce than at present. In this fortunate circumstance I was able to choose an institution that met my requirements. I wished to teach in a small college because of the added opportunities to have personal contacts with the students. I sought a Catholic college because of my desire to link a salaried job with the other important aspects of a life's work. I have been pleased with my choice, King's College.

Not too long ago a professor at another institution, a man whom I respect greatly, asked me, "What exactly are you doing at King's College?" Justify your existence; show how you have fulfilled that early ambition. I cannot, on these terms. Success, fame—and certainly fortune—have eluded me. What have I done, really? Just this: I have tried, I think perhaps about 10 per cent hard, to be a good teacher in a small liberal-arts college for young men.

Even though I am not entirely pleased with my own efforts, I can be pleased with my choice to teach chemistry in a small college. Man, by his nature, is dignified. This dignity comes from two primary sources: the enrichment of the intellect and the development of the will. Of the two, it is easier to enrich the intellect. There are many ways to accomplish this. Of these, I choose to use chemistry because I believe that I am myself able to understand this subject better than any other subject. In teaching chemistry I can play a part in the intellectual development of the individual student; in a small college I can also occasionally help him to know of other equally important subjects. The development of the will I leave to others—I have enough trouble with my own—although in a Catholic college this is not neglected and I am glad to play a minor co-operative role.

As I see it, then, my primary task is to teach a thorough course in chemistry. It is my responsibility, with the able help of my faculty associates, to train a young man to be a chemist first and, almost as important, to help him become a man in the fullest sense of this word.

This task is not alone accomplished by meeting classes and operating a laboratory for the students. Chemistry is a changeable subject. Due to their very nature, the theories concerning the character of matter cannot be known to be true. Often, falsehood masquerades as truth. Oftener, a mixture of falsehood and truth is believed to be true. Little by little, as our understanding of matter increases, we approach closer and closer to what is really true in our theories and in our understanding of the nature of matter. As a consequence, if I wish to teach well, I must be aware of these changes in theories and understanding; failure to maintain the habit of studying the current literature in the field of chemistry will mean failure to teach my students as they should be taught, even at the undergraduate level.

Fortunately, this task, never tedious for one who is interested in the subject, can be made even lighter by a personal intimate interest in any chosen phase of the work that is being performed in this seeking of truth. Although I have not yet succeeded in finding even an unimportant clue to the true nature of matter, I have tried, and it is the attempt that is exhilarating, not the clue itself. In this, and in the other matters mentioned here, I am not different from my colleagues. Few teachers of chemistry have been able to resist the pleasures of research, however small or large their own contributions, or to cite valid reasons for their neglect of this important adjunct to the improvement of their teaching skill.

The present public interest in educational methods and systems has not been confined to collegiate chemistry teaching. It has long been obvious to my colleagues and to myself, however, that we who have specialized in the teaching of chemistry must strive to improve our methods. We must re-examine the curricula, we must improve our techniques. Since improvement in teaching is always possible, to fail to attempt an improvement is to fail to meet a serious obligation. These matters are under continual surveillance by every good teacher of chemistry, at every level, and have been, as testified by published literature, since the early 1920's. Proof is not readily available, but no doubt even before then the same vital interest existed.

A teacher who teaches all he knows is a poor teacher. Three activities—cognizance of current changes in chemistry, personal research and attention to improvement in teaching ability—will help him know more about chemistry than he needs to impart to his students. In addition, maintenance of personal contact with other chemists in industry, in research and in teaching are important. Each of these activities requires that the teacher do more than meet his classes and operate his laboratory courses. Each of these will benefit the students because by these means the teacher is able to enrich his own intellect. And surely, he who asks his students to undertake this enrichment must do so himself.

But of primary importance is the attention given to the individual student. Any teacher, in any subject, can cite instances wherein such help has borne fruit. Students can learn from books, but it is only by personal contact, at the right moment, that they can best be helped to surmount what is to them a stumbling block, whether it be an inability to understand that H_2O, popular opinion to the contrary, is not the formula for water (H_2O is the formula for steam) or whether it be an inability to read and understand what is read. It is even necessary, as is well known, to become a father-confessor, a friend for the moment, a corrector of personality deficiencies. In these matters, of course, skill as well as interest is mandatory in order that a teacher be useful.

Students in difficulty usually have either of two problems: inability to understand simply because they do not make an effort to think, or inability to apply themselves because they are troubled with nonacademic difficulties. In the first case, it is necessary to determine why the student does not try to think. Often he simply may not know that thinking is prerequisite to understanding, or he may be too lazy to undertake the effort. In these cases, the matter is elucidated by simple questioning, with the teacher doing most of the talking—and scolding.

But when the problem is personal, the teacher can usually help best by being silent, merely encouraging the student to speak. If the student knows from the teacher's attitude as exhibited in the classroom that he is speaking to a discreet, interested friend, the teacher need only listen while the student talks to himself. The student's problem, if not solved, is at least then seen in a clearer light.

As a teacher I undertake these tasks for one reason: that my students may excel if they are capable of excellence. Excellence is here defined as a potential ability to contribute something valuable to society (some might prefer to call this creative ability, which would be a good definition). I do not admit to neglect of any student, but I claim a preference for the excellent student. These students, more than others, have the right to expect my personal attention. The others can only be helped a little bit. The excellent student has no limits. In chemistry, and no doubt in other subjects, the excellent student is identifiable by the possession of seven characteristics. First, he has native ability, stifled, perhaps, or enhanced, by his pre-college experiences and schooling. He also tends to work hard, on tasks assigned, without too much regard for his own preferences. His thought is accurate; accurate enough so that, for example, he can catch the inconsistencies of his teachers, not even excepting his chemistry teachers. In addition, he tends to inquire deeply, if water is not H_2O, then what is it? *Exactly* why is *Hamlet* good? What features distinguish the art of Joan Miró from the scribblings of a child? What is wrong, or right, with the foreign policy of this country? Fifth, the excellent student has good reading habits. (One of the most distressing aspects of this matter is the lack of interest exhibited in non-scientific fields by otherwise excellent students. Still it is easier to encourage a student in science to read widely, and well, than it is to interest his non-science classmates in the converse activity. This is perhaps an indictment of our present masters of science and a compliment to all those who have written so well and so interestingly in other fields.) The ability to write well is the sixth criterion of excellence. Without this attribute—the ability to communicate clearly—the fruits of the foregoing abilities will be worthless.

To be classified as excellent, of course, an undergraduate student need exhibit these abilities only in potentiality. I cannot expect to find even one fully developed ability. It is a part of my task, as a teacher of chemistry, to help the student develop these six abilities to a fuller degree.

With the seventh characteristic, moral sensitivity, however, I can do little as a teacher; moral habits depend upon the will, and the will is not easy to manipulate. I expect to find students who do not know why cheating on examinations or in the laboratory is undesirable. There will be some who will disregard the rights of their fellow students. I know of students who have stolen my books or those of their classmates. Yet some of these had the moral sensitivity that is necessary for excellence. To have moral sensitivity is to have well-thought-out reasons, good or bad, for acts that are directly or indirectly related to morality. I would prefer that a student cheat for the wrong reason, as long as that reason seems valid to him, than to cheat for a reason that he knows is poor. What I seek here is evidence of a sensitivity, perverted or acceptable, to the moral implications of an act. Students who first think about their reasons before determining upon a moral act have a greater promise of eventual excellence than those who blithely accept any reason, whether the reason be wrong or right.

A teacher is also required to reflect upon another question. What do I seek to accomplish as a teacher? I certainly cannot give my students all the chemical information they will need in order to become chemists. I do not know all of these things myself. There is not enough time to present this information for their study and attention. Even if I myself knew the necessary information, my knowing does no good. It is the student who must become the knower.

From this I have derived two conclusions: First, it will suffice if the student becomes interested enough to continue to learn. I need only to be sure that he does acquire the elementary background so that he can continue to learn effectively and, as this necessary foundation is acquired, I must at the same time help the student to realize that chemistry is interesting to him. This can be done in many ways, of course. The effectiveness of the methods chosen depends largely upon the personality and individual characteristics of the teacher. In my own case I think I have been least unsuccessful by purposely implying, in my actions and in my words, that *I* think chemistry is interesting and enjoyable.

Chemistry is a broad subject dedicated to an understanding of the material universe. This understanding always begins with a question: Why is grass green? Why does egg white become solid when an egg is cooked? How does waxed paper repel water? Why does gasoline burn? The number of questions is endless and the attempts to find the answers are fascinating, evoking the best intellectual achievements of which man is capable. In an undergraduate course some of these questions can be answered. The student can follow the logic of the answer and take delight in the exercise. This delight is analogous to that felt when a tricky brain-teasing puzzle is solved; but because the questions have a deeper significance than a simple riddle, the delectation is more profound.

The students who are able to attain this enjoyment most readily are those who are naturally disposed toward this kind of intellectual activity. Other students find it less easy to follow the sometimes complicated arguments that lead to the answer, but some appreciation can be developed.

In a word, then, as my first conclusion, I hope to build an attitude that will lead to an eventual intellectual delectation of chemistry by the student.

Second, and I think probably more importantly, it is necessary to recognize that a teacher cannot teach. It is not possible, no matter what tricks are employed, to convey information directly from teacher to student. In the beginning,

I would have affirmed the opposite, vigorously. Bitter experience has indicated that no matter how I may try to cajole, persuade, shout, or plead—no matter how difficult I may make my examinations, the student will not learn from me. Discovery of this fact came as a distinct shock to my ego. I now doubt my ability to teach that a horse has four legs. To teach that all matter is composed of atoms is clearly impossible.

There is a brighter side to this; the best teacher can be a lazy teacher. He simply does not need to try to convey information directly to the student. I can sit back and relax when the student does not learn. It is not possible to force learning in any case.

What I must do is to induce a receptivity. If I am successful, the student will, by a process that I cannot describe, teach himself. The best teacher is indeed lazy if we speak of his disinterest in the direct imparting of information, but he is also a vortex of activity if we speak of his efforts to develop a receptive attitude in his students. In plain words, there are many ways to trick the student into teaching himself. I have tried several, copying from other teachers, devising my own techniques.

In the classroom I develop a topic by calling upon the students at random to recite. The students know the choice is random because they see me pick their names from a set of cards that is shuffled before their eyes. Few wish to appear ignorant in the presence of their classmates and, in addition, the quality of their recitation is recorded. A colleague in another college worked out a scheme for arranging the students according to the excellence of their abilities and then encouraged those lower in the order to challenge those above with questions selected by the teacher or by the student. This method did not work with my classes. Many teachers are opposed to revealing the contents of examination questions before the examination is given because they find that the students study only the questions on the list. I have used this method successfully for several years because I have found that my students do study sufficiently to be able to answer questions that are not on the list. In the laboratory many chemistry teachers distribute substances whose identity is known to the teacher but unknown to the students. By identifying the unknown, the students learn chemistry, and they are eager, under many teachers, to identify these unknown substances. This method has not worked well for me. Instead, I have found that I can promote study by asking questions in the laboratory—when a drinking glass is inverted over a candle flame, why is the flame extinguished?—in order to induce the acquisition of knowledge.

Another feature should be mentioned here. It does not follow, as a conclusion, from my premise that the student must himself become the knower, but it is certainly an essential consideration. This is illustrated by comparing a teacher with a cook. As a teacher I can only present the food to be consumed, in an appetizing manner. If I am successful, the student will consume and, I hope, digest the meal. But it would be a mistake to offer the dessert before the soup. There is an order to these things.

To summarize, these statements are axiomatic. I must whet an interest, an interest that will enable the student to teach himself the elementary matters that I propose to him and that will also be sufficient to inculcate a deeper interest leading to further lifelong study. And I must present in an ordered manner these things by which interest is engendered. Both of these are equal in importance. To fail in either is to fail to teach. Skill in both is necessary and these skills must be constantly improved. To me this is the challenge of teaching. I have found this challenge stimulating and rewarding.

I am sure that I have not yet answered the questions raised in the beginning. Perhaps enough has been said to allow an answer to be drawn from the words, but an overt answer has not been stated. In addition, the question implied in the title to this piece—how can obscurity be accepted?—still remains unanswered.

Why did I become a teacher? I do not really know. I do know that as a creature of God there is, somewhere, a task that I should be performing. I believe that this task is the one I am now carrying out. I could be wrong.

It is obvious that each person is uniquely different from every other person. To me it is also obvious that this implies a different divinely pre-planned task for each person. It is also clear that any individual can reject this task assignment, but this is not pertinent to the theme of the argument. The question is, what is the task assigned to me?

And the answer is, you will never quite be sure what the task is, although you may be reasonably certain.

It might be very nice, although it probably would not work any better than the present system, if God told each and every one of us what our task was to be. If He would give this information directly, a choice could be made—to do His will or to do otherwise. But to me, this attitude smacks of presumption, and therefore will be ineffective; there must be another way for me to learn my assignment.

This other way resides in the concept that every person has an innate ambition, recognizable even to a child or a youth, to accomplish something worth while. This early ambition is a perversion, a mild one, of the real built-in ambition. Instead of the recognized ambition to "do something big," the real innate desire is a desire to become complete, to fulfill an unknown purpose. This innate ambition is improperly interpreted when it is understood as a desire to achieve fame, or fortune, or other worldly accolade.

Sooner or later most of us find that our youthful ambition is not going to be accomplished. We are to be lost, obscure, despite our hopeful attempts to earn a place in history. To me, at least, it has not been pleasant to learn that I could not hope, ever, to realize my earlier ambitions. (So, naturally, it might be said, I now claim the earlier ambition to be a perversion. Perhaps so; but I rather think not.)

If it is true, and I am certain that it is, that my real ambition was to become complete, then this ambition, implanted by God, can be fulfilled by becoming complete only in the way that He has planned. I must know His will in the matter and He will not speak clearly.

Yet, if I have formed the habit of virtue (I make no claim here to have done so; I claim only to have tried), I will have, thereby, become attuned to God's will. I do know what His wishes are in the everyday things. And it is possible that by means of this habit I have also, unknown to myself, become attuned, somehow, to His silent voice in these larger matters, in the choice of my vocation.

Perhaps, in those previous years—when I thought I was seeking fame; when, as I grew, and particularly later on, when I thought I was destined for death on a beachhead, and was tricked into resolving to correct my errors—I was, little by little, learning to do God's will. I was, to put it cynically, becoming pliable, puppet-like. It would be more accurate to say that I am still trying to become pliable, creature-like. I have become a teacher simply because, on my own volition,

I have sincerely tried, not with anything like complete success, even yet, to follow the precepts of God in my everyday life. The rest has been out of my hands.

It may appear that I am not concerned about the difficult problems that confront us in juvenile crime, in racial integration, in the race to the moon. It may appear that I am not as concerned as I should be with the geopolitical problems that are so important today. I do not think that I should help to find a cure for cancer. These tasks have been given to others. I am interested, deeply interested, in these problems; and I hope that solutions will soon be found, but I am not qualified to assist those who seek the answers. My contribution to their work must be indirect. By attending to the problems that confront me, I can best contribute to the solution of these other problems. To be only a good teacher, to do what is morally right (insofar as this is possible), to only cast my vote intelligently at every election and to fulfill my other local civic and social duties is not complacency. It is, rather, a knowledge of limitations; it is a way to find peace of mind.

I can do one task well; I intend to increase my skill in this task. Happily, I believe this task to be the one that conforms to God's will for me. I can best assist others in their tasks by performing my own assignment to the best of my ability. Therefore, though I am deeply interested, I refuse to become concerned about the details of these other important problems.

If I am right, then I will one day complete the only task which is, for me, worth completing. And I may not know, even then, that the task is complete, though I think that I am now engaged in my proper work. But the point is that it does not matter to me that I shall remain obscure; I have found a better goal.

King's College

. . . A Rational Idealism

RICHARD M. EMERSON

PERHAPS the opportunity to publicize my views and feelings about myself, my profession, and my fellow workers should be approached with caution. After all, professional groups are not known for encouraging freedom of expression by way of self-analysis from within their ranks. Maybe this explains why most unrestrained comment-from-within-the-ranks comes as autobiography at retirement. Being at last invulnerable, the long dormant *freedom to express* is invoked as a final catharsis; the soul is cleansed of that spineless "other-directed man." [1]

But I am in no position to view this assignment as a parting shot at the world in which I work. I am thirty-four years old and literally just getting started in academic life, having spent more than twice as much time in preparation than in the work itself. Like most people I am a member of an organization which has at least a loose grip on my career. In short, it might appear that I am as vulnerable, as subject

[1] Yes, I am a sociologist; but since my colleague Mr. Reisman has so successfully coined and popularized the term, I feel I can use it here without being accused of resorting to sociologeeze. Having made this brief apology to Malcolm Cowley, and those who take their cue from him, I will not comment further on special vocabulary.

to censure, as most men, and might with equal justification postpone my comments-from-within until a time approaching retirement. Because this conclusion is erroneous, because the academic world does at least approach some of its own ideals, I am, in fact, free to accept this assignment without that special caution which comes with fear of reprisal, and with no element of special courage involved.

Since I am free to speak about my work and my fellow workers, what devastating things shall I say? That the silent generation fills my classroom? That the organization man walks the college campus under the protective coloration of an academic title, bearing a closer resemblance to Mr. Eliot's Prufrock than to a living, breathing thing? Such assertions are fun to write and read. After all, in perceiving the Prufrock in my associates, I present myself as the man Prufrock wanted to be but lacked the courage to become. Such sweeping indictment or clever profundity is little more than self-flattery for those who write it and for those who, in reading it, accept it as truth.

This is the real reason for the caution I feel in accepting this opportunity to write. When I speak as a professor, I am expected to speak with profundity and I sense that danger lies in *trying* to live up to this expectation. There is a place for profundity in fiction and in the Great Mysteries, but when it is brought with effort into a matter-of-fact description of things, profundity brings fiction and mystery with it. At all cost I will avoid the temptation to appear profound. I assume that a matter-of-fact analysis of me and my kind will be of sufficient interest. After all, you place a large segment of your child's mind in our trust, and you hold us responsible for the development of large segments of "public knowledge" as well. If I can explain how one professor views this responsibility, and how he came to assume it, this should be enough.

We must begin with a simple understanding. I am properly called an academician for only one reason: I work in the academic. Although I am *an* academic man, I am hardly *the* academic man, for like every one of my colleagues in this work I have a few traits I can call my own. A graduate school is not a cookie cutter turning out The Academic Man with each doctorate granted. (Our schools, it is true, have taken on a resemblance to the assembly line, but the result is not uniformly molded men. Rather, if fault is to be found here, it is in the men hardly molded at all.) As people, professors cannot be typed, yet it is the "professorial type" I often encounter in other people's reaction to me. When you see me from a distance, as most of you do, you are likely to see only my professional role and that in a distorted form. If I were introduced to a stranger as a ceramic engineer, the stranger would likely continue to wonder just who and what I am, and proceed further to find out. If introduced as a professor, most would have me sufficiently categorized. Correctly or incorrectly, they feel they know me.

If I am introduced to this stranger as a sociologist, matters are, of course, much worse. Appearing as a guest on a radio panel, I was once introduced to the entire listening audience as "Dr. Emerson, a Socialist at the University of Cincinnati," an error that came as a shock but not as a surprise, knowing that form of the public stereotype from long experience. In the interests of the sponsor and the university I represent, I was forced to devote most of my share of the radio time explaining the "subtle" differences between *socialist* and *sociologist*.

Such misconceptions of the university man, however, do

have their lighter side. A person undergoing psychotherapy can be rude, inconsiderate and in other ways "act out" with impunity; for after all he is *in therapy*. By the same token, a professor can be absent-minded and open-minded. He can drive his car to work and come back on the bus, or he can be so objective as to see two sides to every issue his friends so heatedly discuss. He can even act the intellectual without being so labeled and dismissed. People will understand. They will tolerate his unkempt hair where others go impeccably groomed. Sadly, however, though naturally enough, the public conceptions which make these little freedoms possible come to be shared in part by academicians themselves. Thus, fact takes on a resemblance to fiction. If I take advantage of these little freedoms, I come to resemble the man described as the "professorial type."

Meanwhile, among the more ironic of the little freedoms, available to me as a professor, is the opportunity to be poor with impunity. My failure to achieve wealth is not held against me. I need not apologize for my poverty in any circle. Of course I am underpaid; all professors are, and everyone expects it! It shouldn't surprise you, then, that I feel underpaid myself.

It is nice to be recognized as being worth more than you get, but this small pleasure wears rather thin. One would like to see the difference made up, but here another facet of the professor's public image intervenes. Consider this familiar scene. Whenever I spend a first social evening in the home of a man of means, it is true, I do not have to apologize for my relative poverty. Quite the reverse, he will invariably apologize to me; not for my poverty, mind you, but for his shortage in education and training to "do things really worth doing." These, by inference, are the things I am being paid in: opportunities to do things worth doing. As my host speaks, I slowly see myself more clearly. The, admittedly, lamentably underpaid professor undergoes a slow metamorphosis into the admirable, enviable, devoted man of letters who could not without sacrifice of material things have achieved the finer virtues. Can my host really believe these things? He is on my side all the way, giving me reassurance. What am I to say? Should I deny that I teach for pleasure, not for pay; for the sense of fulfillment which comes with the sight of young minds reaching out to grasp new and broader wisdom? So I nod agreement, and add that *some* work is involved as well. My host then continues his reassurance on the other side of the ledger. The things I have given up or bypassed are not really worth having. Throughout the social evening, woven into casual discussion, my host gives praise for my determination in pursuing and achieving the things-that-money-can't-buy, explaining away the things he bought with money while giving them full display.

In fact, there is no need for any of this! On the one hand, we professors are not so poor as we are assumed to be, and poverty is not a necessary condition for scholarship. On the other hand, I am proud of my training and education, and I enjoy my work. I need no reassurance through praise or apology. My wealthy associate is equally proud of the success his wealth represents, and with equally good reason. I'll flaunt my academic title, if you will flaunt your indicator of success, whatever it may be. Then, with this kind of understanding, if you still feel the professor is in general underpaid, don't apologize; endow a chair, or vote properly on bond issues. Apologies are suspect.

Meanwhile, academicians, on the whole, agree that they

are underpaid. While, in part, this may be derived from your apologies, it is nonetheless consistent with any standard I can think of. Of course there are some who do not fully earn the small amount they receive. If there are devoted professors, as my host assumes, they have their apathetic counterparts as well. Inquire into the sources of apathy, however, and you will likely find the opportunity for proper recompense among them. Hence, as a *group,* professors are underpaid.

I can't really argue with my host on these points. While by most standards we view ourselves as underpaid, we feel that academic life is worth it. Hence, our efforts to improve our lot do not often take us out of academic life. There is no great exodus of professors into industry and government. Meanwhile, there is some disagreement among us as to how we might best improve our lot.

One of my colleagues at the lunch table argues that we should face realities. We are employees, hired *by* administrators to work *for* and *under* administrators. The notion that a university is a curriculum controlled by a faculty, with administrator-clerks hired to do the paper work and bookkeeping, is all part of the professor's fantasy life. Since no one else shares that fantasy, my colleague argues, we border upon the psychotic in holding to it. We should recognize our status as employees and unionize like any other self-respecting working group. However, across the table, and between puffs on his pipe, another professor soberly shakes his head. Such action is not befitting the dignity of the academic *profession.*

So one man sees us as "workers" who sacrifice self-interest to fancied respectability. He is correct also. We are workers pretty much as he describes within the organization of the university, and we do so sacrifice. The other man views us as professional men with dignity and respectability to lose. He is absolutely correct. That is just what we do stand to lose. Hence, these men may debate the point indefinitely and without resolution; for, in fact, we are workers receiving professional respectability as a fringe benefit. In the organization of the university we are employees, while in the organization of our respective fields, from astronomy to zoology, we are professional men and like very much to view ourselves as such.

I side with the man of dignity against unionization, but I hasten to add that dignity is not the point of the issue. Rather it is efficacy. A union is a group joined by shared circumstances and a workable strategy. We share the circumstances in some respects, but for us the strategy would not work. Demand a larger share of what profits? Strike against whom? Rather than acting like self-respecting workers, we should take our professional affiliations more seriously and improve our lot just as most other professional groups protect theirs. We should tighten up on admittance standards into the academic professions, restrict our own numbers and make our scarcity felt. We should, through justified achievement standards, put some respectability back into the Ph.D. Here, too, prices can be controlled in part through the control of production. The academic world is plagued with overproduction in its graduate schools and should seize the opportunity to stabilize production and in so doing guarantee the quality of the product.

Of course, there are no important signs of such action at present. Schools are finding all kinds of ways to increase their graduate programs, to turn out greater quantities and more kinds of "Doctors." One dean, introducing a new program, put it down very clearly for all to hear: "I am interested in *numbers,* mind you, *numbers!*" (Italics are his.) The statement did help, however, in arousing widespread demand among the faculty for an appraisal of doctoral programs in general throughout the institution.

While I would like to expand on this theme at length, I will leave it to you for now to reason out the pros and cons of such a recommendation in terms of the interest of any group involved, including the general public of today, tomorrow and the next day. In your analysis, keep in mind that Ph.D.'s, by and large, have no special training as teachers of undergraduate students, and your child has no special need for a Ph.D. as his teacher at that level. Go still further and carry out an analysis of the job the academician is charged with, the process of recruitment and the kind of man recruited under given conditions.

The "underpaid professor," while discomforting as fact, is pleasing as a public image. The most prevalent public conception of all, however, is meant to be derogatory. This stereotype, too, has its factual basis, but in this case it is heavily distorted. I refer to the image of the professor as a *man-removed-from-life;* a picture of the man which comes in many themes and variations. He lives in an ivory tower, sheltered, in retreat from the demands, responsibilities and decisions of mortal men. He does not live a life, he analyzes other people's lives. He elevates every topic to abstract unreality, failing to perceive or respond to the concrete and immediate events about him. He thinks, but does not feel. He talks, but does not do. Being so removed from things, he is inept and bumbling, unable to manage his own life. It follows then, that someone must dominate and care for him: his wife if he has one.

Some form of this misconception is found in virtually every corner of our population. I found it in the thinking of a very eminent and capable poet during an evening's discussion of his work: The universities are killing poetry in America! The professor of poetry and literature "thinks" about a poem, analyzes it before students, and criticizes it in print. Beauty is not a thing of the intellect, to be dissected and explained with conceptual scalpels. Aestheticians spin theories to account for the aesthetic experience of others. They are rendered incapable of the experience themselves through their own diagnostic habits of mind. The aesthetician is the artist's academic counterpart.

Throughout this artist's appraisal of things run impossibly tangled threads of truth and fiction. Poetry is read with passion by students and professors alike, while being discussed as well. The aesthetician is fully capable of shedding tears, and no doubt does, partly because of his analytic habits of thought. I hold this to be true in all fields: intellectual comprehension enhances appreciation at every level, including the aesthetic.

Some of the things that I appreciate most for sheer beauty are high alpine mountains, their winding valley glaciers and foreboding corniced ridges. I love to feel them beneath my feet, when climbing, as well as view them as a painter might. As a college sophomore midway in the development of this appreciation, I enrolled in a series of courses in geology taught by one of our academicians. There I learned about the mountains. From textbooks, lectures and field trips devoted to analysis, I discovered the processes which bring mountains into being. Technical terms and concepts were employed in abundance to cut apart, to dissect and analyze, the things I was coming to love. I came to love them all the more in the process. Thanks to academicians, who may or may not have shared my appreciation for the mountains, the "purely intellectual" concept of geologic time now accompanies me on every climbing expedition.[2] Can anyone, then, look me in the eye and tell me that my knowledge of the mountain stands as a barrier between me and the full beauty it possesses? As I ascend the mountain I can now read from its contours its past and its future, and my climb is placed in grand context. In fact, through the whole experience I am placed in context! And, mind you, people ask me why I climb mountains.

So, what is there of value in the academic (that is "non-practical, removed-from-life") study of a topic? People ask this question, too. Such questions are difficult to answer because those who ask have never climbed a mountain and have no interest in a topic. I say *they* are far removed from life.

The eminent poet can be matched with an even more eminent writer of fiction in holding the misconception of the man-removed-from-life. In *Point of No Return,* J. P. Marquand paints a picture of the social anthropologist as one who, having no life of his own, lives vicariously through the lives of people in the community he is studying. I suspect that he is representing the findings of an anthropologist known for his study of status relationships. I would not be surprised if Marquand derived the inspiration for the novel directly from these studies, for *Point of No Return* is 100 per cent sociology in its content and I have my students

[2] The concept of geologic time is about as far removed from direct intuitive experience as an idea can be. It is a purely rational construction in its origin and use as a geologist's intellectual tool. It is intended as an aid in rational comprehension rather than profound emotion. Yet the concept inevitably provides both, and the latter in a form unattainable without the concept.

read it as such. Every insight the novel contains, presented in artistic or fictional form, is contained in the common statements of sociological writing. Even so, the writer-as-artist can seldom afford to admit the validity of social and psychological concepts. Concepts tend to remove the profundity from his work. They make his insights commonplace.

Thus, the artist's attack upon academic analysis boils down to the simple assertion that it is not art. And, of course, it isn't. To illustrate, Gertrude Stein once wrote: "I know that I am I because my little dog knows me. But who am I when my little dog dies?" A social psychologist translates the same insight into such notions as "taking the attitude of the other toward the self," "significant others" and "ego-involvement." In the translation, the poetry, the concrete imagery, is lost; but the concept remains valid, and it helps in grasping the poem.

My argument with the misconception can be carried to areas other than poetry and the aesthetic. As a sociologist I am called upon to "analyze" group conflict among other topics. Like the geologist, it is my job to accomplish intellectual comprehension in the course of such analysis. My efforts lead me, as they do him, through special terminology; some very simple notions such as the "in-group"; other concepts, such as "culture," which are much more difficult to properly conceive and convey than is "geologic time"; but all devoted to making the behavior of men in groups understandable. The analysis is intended to remove the Mysteries from man's conduct, and with them the fantasies men devise to explain the Mysteries.

With all of this, I find myself lecturing, let us say, on war. Now, the stereotype takes the analytic "jargon" and the "man-removed-from-life" and asks: What does he know about real war? War occurs out here, in life. He, the professor, coolly talks about war. What we really have to do is *fight* them and *win* them, and then proceed to analyze them in the academy. An academician makes war academic! Well, yes and no, as we shall see.

In fact, as a professor of sociology lecturing on war, I am in a position to view the phenomenon in a most unprofessorial way, while it is precisely my students who are not able to do so. From Leghorn to Lake Garda, through the Apennine Mountains and across the Po Valley of Italy, there is a long string of foxholes. I dug them, and I still have a fond feeling for them. Any hole in the ground will acquire the sentiments of home when you have such total dependence upon it; when you can attribute continued life to its sunken form. I even developed a love for the M-1 rifle. Whoever heard of an academician fondly rubbing a walnut rifle stock with linseed, protectively guarding his sight-setting against sudden knocks; actually in anger and fear trying to kill with the thing! Imagine the stereotyped professor you hear lecturing on war crouched in a German dugout opposite its freshly killed occupant, eating the dead German's lunch with a peace of mind derived directly from his death (and the protection his death provided).

My purpose, of course, is not to tell war stories here, and they never enter my lectures as such. They simply point out that if war is part of life, your professor is by no means removed from same. My students fully realize this without need for personalized battle accounts. At the time of these events, however, I was not a professor; only a nineteen-year-old soldier with a faint aspiration toward the academic. If those circumstances were to be repeated, I would feel quite differently about them, due to my age, the family I now have, etc. The fact that I have since become an academician—specifically a sociologist, with whatever habits of mind that entails—would also bring certain alterations in my reactions. Unavoidable tragedy would crowd out some of the glory and drama; a little compassion would disturb that peace of mind. Meanwhile I would proceed as before to check my sights and take food when and where I could.

It may seem unfair to attribute this broadened appreciation of a war event to academic life and training. As it happens I wrote a short story (never published) some years after the event, entitled "Perverted Peace of Mind." My peace of mind at the time was a perfectly natural reaction and certainly not perverted. Only under reflection and analysis does it appear so. While such reflection, such analytic appraisal, is thankfully not restricted to the academic, it is the academician's business to reflect. In any case, as a man-removed-from life, I have had the chance to reflect upon such episodes of "living." As a result, I feel I partly comprehend the German and the social processes which brought him to his death in that hole in the ground. I am completely unable to view him as a man in any way different from me. The demon I was trained to see in him and his kind is gone, and with it goes the hate. But not the fear. The forces at work might be comprehended, but they are not controlled. Hence, the situation demanded his death (he had neither the will nor the opportunity to surrender), and *comprehension* of the situation makes the death tragic, puts compassion in the killing.

These few feelings, on war and mountains, and the poetry involved in both, are small samples of my personal property. They belong to *me,* not to *the academic man.* The simple understanding I hope we can come to is that the academician is not a man at all. It is a role, a form of conduct expected of and performed by those people like myself whom you call professors, in the limited context of learning and teaching what is learned. Once you recognize it as a role and not a type of person, you can then realize that the academic role really exists as something more than a misguided stereotype of "the professor." It exists in your expectations of me; and during those hours when I live up to your expectations, in my research and teaching, it exists in my actions. Beyond this, "the professor" does not exist at all.[3]

So I am neither absent-minded nor open-minded. But I do work in the academic setting and there I am expected to engage in intellectual analysis. In this sense I, as an example, may be removed-from-life. As a one-time student of geology I was not out digging gold, or otherwise seeking direct monetary return. When I want to understand group conflict, including wars, I have to do more than fight. I have to stand back and reflect upon them, momentarily removed from this facet of living. And if you wish to avoid wars, you will do well to understand them.

I have gone out of my way to emphasize that my colleagues and I are persons, not types. Having made this point, I can now admit that there is a certain sameness among us. In one respect, at least, I am very much like the majority of academicians. Any similarities I have with most of my fellow workers, however, can be traced to the impact which the academic environment has had upon them and me alike. And it

[3] This simple understanding may be applied to any instance of stereotyped thinking. For example, the "organization man" whom we have come to know so intimately does not exist as a type of person. Mr. Whyte was not observing the man so much as the organization, and viewed in this manner his observations have a great deal of validity. Otherwise they are most confusing. Release the organization man from his dependence upon the organization, or view him in a different social context, and the label will not fit.

has had its impact. Tied in closely with the intellectual analysis involved, there is an underlying philosophy or world view. It is my own personal view of things, but I join so many other academicians in adhering to it that it is best thought of as part of the academic atmosphere. Some professors bring this world view with them, in which case it is an important factor leading them into academic life. Others have absorbed it from the university setting. Both were true in my own case.

This underlying philosophic theme comes to the surface in many variations, and some of these have been named. In the area of personal moral conduct, for example, it comes out in elaborated form as Humanism. Perhaps I am a Humanist. Many men on our campuses are. In some areas of study it comes in a highly disciplined form called Science and in some of my work I am a scientist. If I am going to speak of a philosophic thread which joins me, a sociologist, with many of my colleagues in biology, chemistry, moral philosophy, aesthetics and literature alike, I must name that thread. *Science* or the *Scientific Attitude* is too confining. *Determinism* is close, but carries with its notions of *pre*determinism and a fatalistic attitude which do not belong to the world view I see in myself and those about me. I would call it *Naturalism,* although it is too simple and casual to be an *ism* at all. It is the simple faith that for every event, be it a falling apple or an act of sin, there is a perfectly *natural* explanation.

A natural explanation is an accounting which invokes no special powers or forces to account for things. Thus, Naturalism is distinct from *super*naturalism. Furthermore, this faith permits no exemptions, no *special* events which defy explanation. Thus, Naturalism is distinguishable from mysticism. In this world view, nothing is mysterious, extraordinary or unique. Anything can be accounted for as a case covered by natural principles, if and when those principles are formulated.

These are the simple assumptions which I and so many of my colleagues work upon. It is the business of the academician to formulate and teach natural principles in their respective fields. No wonder, then, that this naturalistic world view is so prevalent on the college campus. Every imaginable topic of interest is being studied as a natural phenomenon in some corner of our universities, from the nature and origin of "life" and "morality," to the mechanisms producing harelip in the house mouse. While to some people "beauty" is a completely ineffable experience capable only of being enjoyed, to the aesthetician it is a "thing" to be analyzed and explained. In this approach to beauty he is a naturalist, just as much as Charles Darwin was a naturalist in his study of animal forms. Some people conceive of the Devil to account for the sin in man's conduct, and God to account for man's morality. As a sociologist, however, I am bound to view such things as sin and morality as by-products of group life in the most everyday earthly sense. In this my approach is naturalistic. A sociologist is a naturalist. (He may or may not be a scientist as well, but I will not go into such distinctions here.)

Most people's world contains a segment held immune from natural inquiry, while in other segments such inquiry is the order of the day. These segments are the *sacred* and the *profane* respectively. For the full-blown naturalist nothing is sacred. I am prepared, for example, to treat human values, even the gods people worship, as man-made earthly products, traceable to the demands of group living. While such things inevitably command my profound respect, I do not treat them as sacred, as exempt from natural inquiry. Instead, I study them as aspects of animal behavior—the human animal—and no topic can be more fascinating or more worthy of study.

It does not surprise me, however, that you consider this simple philosophy of mine as rather obvious, lacking the profundity which philosophies should possess. After all, it is a philosophy of the *profane,* of the everyday aspects of life such as the steaming kettles in our kitchens. More properly, it is a profane way of viewing things, for it classifies the ritual performances in our temples alongside those kettles as "things" to be examined. This is inevitably a profane point of view, for when natural inquiry is turned upon things held sacred, it tends to remove their mysteries—and the fantasies men devise to explain the Mysteries. In so doing, it makes things appear profane or commonplace, and for this it is feared.

As a sociologist, it is my business to engage in natural inquiry into man and the institutions which shape his conduct. As a result I frequently examine things which many people prefer to leave unexamined; but there is no cause for fear or alarm about this work. Analysis does not turn morality into anarchy! Through such analysis some have discovered, for example, the idea of "cultural relativity"; the notion that moral codes, being man-made, are relative to time and place rather than universal and absolute. It is true that some people read anarchy into this doctrine; but only if they have not themselves carried out the analysis involved, thereby failing to appreciate the functional value, the basic respectability, of *any* set of codes. People sense anarchy in this idea only if their personal morality is so shaky as to require *absolute doctrine* for support. Such support is always on the verge of collapse.

Still others embrace the notion of cultural relativity because of the anarchy they see in it. This is the reaction of an adolescent mind seeking freedom from restraining moral codes. Such a person has come by the doctrine secondhand. He has acquired it from a very poor teacher.

A proper comprehension of such relativism will not of necessity undermine the validity of your codes. Rather, it will permit you to appreciate the validity of other codes in the lives of other people. It leads one down a one-way street to tolerance. Thus, when Naturalism is applied to human conduct, a more pervasive philosophy develops. Instead of anarchism, the derivative philosophy is Humanism. Humanism is the outgrowth of natural inquiry applied to men.

It is by no means safe to argue that all men in the academic hold the naturalistic world view I describe, but if there is any feature of sameness among us, it is this mental outlook. The academic institution fosters such a faith; indeed, it is founded upon it.

Like many others, however, I brought an incipient form of Naturalism with me into the academic. In fact, my choice of this career can be attributed in large part to the circumstances which funneled my thinking into a primitive form of natural inquiry long before I encountered sociology and academic life.

In looking back at those circumstances, I make the same discovery that Marcel Proust made in his *Remembrance of Things Past:* happenings take on more meaning when viewed in retrospect. At the moment we feel that we act and decide with passion and conviction. But, viewed from a position far removed, with context provided by precedent and outcome, those passions and convictions seem only to implement what circumstances made inevitable. Looking back, we see for the first time the all-important circumstances. Thus, we choose our careers, for example, much as a stream of water selects its course—governed by the shape of the particular terrain we live in. You will see that I did not "choose" the academic at all. I was moved along toward it by a pattern of circumstances of which I was unaware at the time. When we do not know why a person did what he did, we say he "chose" to do it. Natural inquiry into human conduct tends to remove the element of "choice" in its usual sense. In fact, the doctrine of "free will" exists largely as a tribute to our ignorance about the nature of human behavior. I want to know *why* I became an academician, and I am not content to drop the matter by saying simply that I "decided" to be one.

If my parents and immediate family had been the good and solid Mormons that my friends' families were, my personality today would be eternally humble, self-effacing and self-righteous. Some of my friends think they see a trace of those qualities in me now, but they should see the me who might have been. That is the kind of person *some* Mormons are, and it is the kind of Mormon I was rapidly becoming. Furthermore, such a Mormon could not possibly be a sociologist. With no reflection upon his native endowments whatever, he would be a failure from the start. He would be as uncomfortable and out of place in sociology as I was in Mormonism; and he would soon drop my faith, as I did his.

I trace my entry into sociological study to the peculiar nature of my departure from Mormondom. My break from this neatly circumscribed way of life stamped a naturalistic view of group life into my mental make-up. It developed a clumsy form, but it was there long before I heard of sociology. Academic training simply polished it up a bit to make me presentable among other sociologists.

Meanwhile, the events which crowded me into academic life formed their pattern early.

I was born in a Mormon family consisting of grandfather, grandmother, two uncles, two aunts and a mother. Long before my arrival, Grandfather's Mormonism was converted to intense cynicism toward the Church organization and its people, with whom he had no further contact. The events involved in this conversion make a fascinating tale too long to go into here. It is sufficient to know that he was completely isolated from the Church, while continuing to study its doctrine as a self-styled theologian. Meanwhile, I was raised in the very humble house he rented, and I love him. Hence, he must have loved me.

Grandfather's cynicism tempered the Mormonism of all family members into apathetic, liberal or cynical forms. His wife, trying to balance the forces, grew apathetic. His oldest son, being closest to him, became completely cynical. The rest of the family were liberal Mormons at the time I arrived. My mother had been further weakened by a marriage outside the faith, a marriage which dissolved soon after my birth, placing both of us back in the home. By the time I arrived in this family, conflicting forces had formed an equilibrium of hushed silence. I never heard Mormonism discussed in the home, pro or con, and it was never practiced as a family affair. Those of you who know Mormonism know how unique this is. I was left to find my way as best I could in these matters, and my way was into the Church through friends and their families.

From the time I was five years old until I entered the service in 1943, my relationship to the Mormon Church was that of an adopted child. I know this now. I only felt it then.

At five, I formed a close and long friendship with the son of the Ward Bishop, later Stake President, Mission President, and a man still rising in the Church. Through this friendship I was drawn into the Church and into my friend's family as a single process. The result: I felt like a visitor in both.

Worst of all, I was made to feel like an underprivileged visitor, receiving the protection of spiritual love from those who have a surplus in same. This sounds cruel, I know, for my friend and his family, his father high in the Church, were and are the most sincere and well-intentioned people one can find. I knew that then, and I know it now, but that does not change these childhood feelings one bit. This family's complete sincerity, and my knowledge of it did little more than postpone and soften my inevitable break from their way of life. More important, as you will see, their sincere acceptance of me was a critical piece in the pattern which led me into my present line of work. Meanwhile, I attended church, participating as Mormons participate, but wondering all the while just what I was doing there. I heard others profess their belief and testify to the warmth and strength it gave them. I "believed," but I could find no warmth involved. I felt truly like a stranger in the midst of people who appeared to care about me.

One or two little events can be used to portray a thousand episodes of this period, for they all carry the same message. My friend's father wanted his son to have a seasonal membership at the gymnasium, there to "learn to swim and grow strong." Knowing that his son would want to swim with me; assuming that my mother could not afford such a membership; in his fatherly way, he called us before him offering to buy memberships for both. He purchased one for his son, but I was not big enough at that time to accept. I resented the kindness of his offer. This was one of many little things that built the sense of my adopted status in this family and the Church it stood for. It weakened my friendship with his son as well as my attachment to his church.

The full nature of my relationship to Mormonism, however, is seen in a later event occurring when I was thirteen. I was included, with a few other Boy Scouts, on a vacation taken by this family. The trip took us to a Mormon community in Canada. To the many people they knew there, I was always introduced, with a hand on my shoulder: "And this is Dick Emerson. He is Andrew Parratt's grandson. You remember Andrew Parratt." There the words stopped, but the meaning continued in their manner: "But you see, we treat him like a son, for we are proper people, and through our grace he may become the same. Already he is a fine, humble lad, worthy of being introduced." My mind missed this unintended meaning, but my thirteen-year-old emotions could not fail to grasp it. I was a second-class citizen in this Mormon world—no doubt about it. There is, in fact, the essence of caste in Mormondom, though obscured behind a surface ethic of universal brotherhood.

These people were so thoroughly kind and accepting toward me that I could not attribute my sense of alienation to them. All I knew was that in their presence I felt like a permanent guest, while with others I felt a little more like a person able to accept guests. I thank Circumstances for providing those others! But for the presence of gentiles in the Salt Lake Valley, I would have been the would-have-been-me I described. Instead, I was able to change from Mormon to sociologist only because of the coincidental presence of gentiles and the qualified Mormonism of my family. So the stream flowed, with slow meanders, out of Mormon country and into gentile territory. I remained a member of the

Church, but gentiles could be counted among my associates in increasing numbers.

After a few months in the service, the terminal event arrived. My mother passed away after a short life of hard work, and I rushed home on leave. Arrangements had been made. My friend's father would speak at my mother's funeral. Most proper! But what could he possibly say? To my knowledge he had never met my mother. Their lives were held rigidly apart by translucent lines of caste. I was the only link between them, and I had to be two very different people to form the link. The whole episode seemed to symbolize the immense gulf, the *cleavage* of caste, which separated me from these exceedingly kind and righteous people. The event placed me so precariously astride this line that I was bound to tumble.

So my mother's funeral was devoted to me. She was eulogized through praise of the son she bore and raised. While she didn't attend church she was, by inference, a fine woman anyway, for her son is a fine young man, possessing all the Mormon virtues. Many in the audience were brought to tears. I was brought into total confusion. On the morning of the funeral, if someone had put the question to me directly, I would not have been able to say whether I was a Mormon or not. It might have depended upon who asked. I couldn't hope to analyze my state of mind after this funeral speech, but one thing became clear for the first time in my life: I was not a Mormon, and I doubted that I ever had been.

I should have fled, but instead I approached my friend's father immediately after the service to thank him for his participation. In response, he invited me to go through Temple rites with his son. (He was high enough in the Church to extend this unusual offer.) But I didn't have one fraction of the moral strength required to refuse the offer of this man who had spoken with such sincerity in my (or my mother's?) behalf, to tell this man that I was no longer a member of his church. These Circumstances came too fast upon each other.

So at week's end my friend and I went side by side through the most sacred and restricted Mormon rites, but the forces impelling us were vastly different. For my friend the ceremony stood, no doubt, as a memorable moment, signalling his attainment of maturity in the Mormon faith; yet for him the event was simply part of a sequence, fixed in the prior nature of things, as predictable as the moon maturing toward fullness. He reaffirmed the beliefs he had always held, and he dedicated himself to a way of life which had firmly gripped him from the time of his conception. Every feature of his make-up, every facet of his life, gave him reason to submit, to be fully consumed in the sacred rites. Thus, for my friend the stage was set for a religious experience.

For me, however, the stage was set for a first sociological insight. I entered the Mormon Temple as an outsider and the ceremonies were strange and distant things to be *observed* with respectful curiosity. But I was in no state of mind to observe these rites with the detached eye of a visiting anthropologist. A month later I could not even remember the ceremonies I had vowed never to reveal. I was by no means a man-removed-from-life, taking field notes during this trip through the Mormon Temple. Having abandoned the well-defined patterns of Mormonism, I was a man without a context, and during my passage through the stages of the Temple ceremony I had been launched into anxious wondering. I had to know *why*—why I was there, and why my friend and I perceived the same ceremony as two quite different things. It was not long before I realized that my friend was a devout

Mormon because social circumstances provided no alternative; that I left the Church because social circumstance had not permitted me to fully join it. I soon realized that I did not "decide" to leave the Church and in an act of will depart. On the first occasion when I really looked, I simply "discovered" that I was on the outside looking in. I can date my discovery of my gentile character to the day of my mother's funeral, but my actual departure from the Mormon faith cannot be dated. It did not take place as an act, a decision or an event. It was woven into the fabric of all the social relations I was ever involved in, Mormon and non-Mormon alike.

This was my first insight into the social forces operating in a person's conduct, and it came well before I had heard of sociology. The whole experience, I believe, prepared me to receive the naturalistic approach of sociology without resistance, and I entered the field with excitement. The sociology of religion is now only a small segment of my interest.

Perhaps my account has led you to believe that I am, indeed, a man-removed-from-life as professors are often thought to be. It is certainly true in my case that a naturalist's view of things ordinarily considered sacred was made possible by my feeling of separateness from a faith held by others. But there is more to it than that. The detachment I developed regarding Mormonism had not the slightest resemblance to the cold, sterile observation attributed in stereotype to academicians. A student of nature, it is true, does not worship plants and animals, but he loves them in a special way nonetheless. Our biologists are frequently numbered among our conservationists as a result, for after all, they do *care*. In a similar way I feel an abiding fondness for Mormonism and for Mormons in particular. But I worship neither, and for this reason I am able to make at least an honest effort to understand them as they are. Neither Mormon nor militant anti-Mormon can make this claim. Neither is in a position to comprehend Mormonism as it really is. Thus, "professorial detachment" does exist, but, seen in its true perspective, it is nothing more than the naturalistic viewpoint I have illustrated in my own case. Furthermore, this kind of detachment brings its own special virtues. The respect and regard I now feel for Mormons is a direct by-product of the naturalistic view I take toward their way of life. How often do you find this in expatriates from *any* group?

Many ex-Mormons, in the process of losing faith, commence to study Mormonism, but their study is framed to refute and belittle. A sociological perspective prevented me from doing this. Instead, I inquired into the origin of their institutions and beliefs, and the meaning they derive from believing. How could I develop anything but a profound respect for their forms of living? In the process, however, I believe I discovered some truths about group life which are equally valid in any group. Now, my friend who remained in the Church surely knows (or feels) what *believing* means in his life, but he considers this to be unique to Mormonism. He has failed to grasp the general truths contained within his own faith because he was never given the chance to step back into professorial detachment and examine that faith. He remains, as a result, self-righteous, intolerant of the ways of others.

Such intolerance is incompatible with a sociological perspective, which sees a man and his actions as things of nature, fully accounted for in his conditions of living. In fact, I'll go even further. What we know as Christian compassion and forgiveness are automatically contained in the almost deterministic assumptions of Naturalism, summarized in the assertion: *There, but for the grace of Circumstance, go I.* The compassion I feel in retrospect for a dead German soldier, and the regard I feel for Mormons with whom I could not continue to live, can be offered as bits of evidence.

Thus, when my sociology spills over from the classroom and the research design, out into the affairs of life, it emerges as a form of Humanism. But in this I confess I am less than perfect, for occasionally I meet someone I cannot help but despise. Perhaps that makes me human, if you choose to put it that way. Meanwhile, as a sociologist it is not my objective to spread human understanding about in the world. I am simply bent on understanding the make-up of men and groups of men, and I have a long way to go in this direction before I will call a halt and start militantly applying what I *think* I have learned.

University of Cincinnati

. . . The Education Counselor

SHEPARD A. INSEL

I AM reasonably certain that people are not born to do special things, though I'm aware that there are inherited characteristics, which, when fused together and encouraged to develop, produce what we like to call "talent." Even so, the presence of talent doesn't necessarily decide for a person what he is going to do in life. Rather, it seems to me, that our social systems determine in a very complicated manner the kind of activities which are seen as desirable, and if we are strongly identified with our cultures, our energies are aimed at goals consistent with their values. For example, our growing children go through a series of phases when they sequentially plan to become milkmen, firemen, cowboys, nurses, doctors, and the other actively participating working roles seen around them.

But if we merely examine the chronology of our developing identification with those in the world around us, what becomes our eventual work discipline or professional activity seems to have little relation to the daily experiences of our earlier years.

Certainly, my past history doesn't clearly account for my being a member of a college faculty today. As a matter of fact, becoming a college professor was probably the last thought anyone in my family could have had for me, especially myself. It was primarily the circumstances of World War II, with the attendant social upheaval, which determined the academic pattern of my life, and resulted in my doing psychological counseling.

In the first place, the thoughtful, systematic, somewhat mild style of life led by the stereotypical college professor had little place in my immediate family's existence. We were oriented toward action, physical work, making a living, for I grew up during the period of the depression in a family whose existence was marginal.

In the second place, I don't recall having contact at a social level with people who were college trained. My teachers, the doctor, the dentist—all seemed to be beyond our social sphere, and they were treated with the deference accorded people who were heroes. I remember the pride I took in the knowledge that my best friend's older brother went to college at night, studying to become an engineer. It was as if he were my own blood relative. Obviously, the status of the college-trained person existed in my family's values. Indeed, as a child my father would introduce me to his friends with the added statement that he would be sending me to college some day.

If anybody in my family had the makings of a scholar, it was my mother's father. He was a gentle, devout Jew, who had somewhat retreated from the rough-and-tumble existence of an uneducated Lithuanian immigrant of the early 1900's. During his later years, he turned to his religion in a most scholarly manner, as a teacher of Hebrew to young boys who were being made ready for their religious confirmation.

He had suffered greatly from the torments of religious and social persecution, and had found solace from a passive, contemplative life, existing with his family on a minimal income in New York. Though he had had no formal education, he was nevertheless considered a learned man by his friends and neighbors. It was he who set the tone of respecting the educated man in my family.

I was my grandfather's only grandson during my early years, and as such, I received a great deal of attention from him. He was always very good to me, but I'm afraid we didn't understand each other very well. He taught me many things in the Hebrew tradition, and I learned to read and write the liturgical language at an early age. However, I was a very active child, and I resented the demands he made on my playtime. But he had the final authority in my family and received the support of my parents. As a result, I probably spent about double the time studying that my friends and playmates did. I sometimes suspect that this pressure to study at such an early age led to my rebelling against study later on. Nevertheless, this core of learning experience may also have established the basis for my later work in psychology, for much of Talmudic scholarship involves the behavior of men in their relations with each other.

My mother incorporated the gentle nature of her father into herself, and also some of his unobtrusive persistence in living through the daily struggle. Though life to her means the bearing of social responsibility, she has some of the optimist in her outlook, and she expresses quiet enthusiasm and warmth for the new and the exciting. Perhaps it is this aspect of her which allowed—no, directed—her to find a relationship with my father.

What my mother's family style of life was, my father's was not. There was nothing passive or contemplative about his family's approach to life, and he as the eldest of seven children, eloquently represented that style. For he was a strong, restless, gregarious, impulsive person, who generally expressed impatience toward indecision. His design for living provoked crisis, and it was as though he enjoyed nothing better than the taste of battle. My recollections of his values during my earlier years point toward expressions of strength and handicraft skills, though he had had little formal training.

As a child I idolized and feared my father. He always seemed to be so capable, and was sought after by many people to help them with their problems, both mechanical and political. But he was also very demanding and impatient with me. I recall trying to help him dig a ditch when I was about eight years old; having difficulty with the man-sized shovel, I excavated unevenly. Seeing this, he grabbed the shovel away, saying, "You'll never be able to work with your hands. You'd better become a college professor." These prophetic words could hardly have a causal value, but my recollection of them attests to the amount of meaning the incident had for me, and the attitude my father held toward unhandy people.

However, even though as a child I felt I was never able to live up to my father's standards, I apparently meant a great deal to him, for as I think about it, I spent a great amount of time going places with him, helping him with his many little side activities, for he was the original do-it-yourself-man. Nevertheless, I suspect that my striving to be accepted by him, my feeling of being constantly misunderstood by him, made me painfully sensitive to the extent to which people can misperceive each other. The welling up of the feeling of futility when a dependent person reaches out for tenderness and understanding and meets with what is construed as harshness, is no doubt a well-known emotional experience for many of us. These experiences with my father helped me to become aware of the struggles young people have in growing up to fulfill themselves in their relations with others, though it was much later in my life that I achieved any insight into the meanings of the experiences. Also much later, during the war, my father, who was in the Air Force, wrote me a very poignant letter just prior to embarking on a dangerous secret mission overseas, in which he confessed his awareness that he had always been unable to express his loving, encouraging feelings to his children. It is interesting that as a grandfather now, he is quite capable of communicating his warm affection to my children.

My mother was inclined to be permissive and quite accepting of others, even when she knew she should be firm and unyielding. Toward my younger brother and sister and myself, she was always supportive, and I cannot recall any experience when she uttered a harsh word in our direction. Her capacity to absorb stress is still a wonder to us, and her example has been of major value in my learning to live and work with the personal problems of others.

Both my parents have respected education as a utility through which to make something of oneself. But neither could have been called studious in outlook. This, coupled with the fact that both represented different temperaments, had differing values and forms of expression, resulted in my having mixed and frequently conflicted feelings about education.

It seems to me, then, that I had much of my mother's sensitivity, but sought to pattern myself after my father, and I was involved at every turn with reconciling two broad, conflicting aspects of myself. Though I am unable to recall specifically, I was no doubt a very inconsistent person during my growing-up period, and to paraphrase Thomas Mann, I've had to learn how to live with the many mutual contradictions within myself.

In this respect, I find that many conflicts expressed by students seeking counseling center around their frustrated desires to eradicate features within themselves which they cannot tolerate. To do so, however, is to deny one's past, sometimes at a loss to a developing integrity. For example, a student whose desire is to appear adequate in the eyes of those around him, becomes fearful that he will expose his uncertainties if he expresses himself, and so he remains quiet to the extent that he is unable to utilize the social opportunities to develop the very sense of adequacy he seeks.

But while my own inconsistent development had its drawbacks, mainly in the lack of my forming a disciplined approach to situations, I also had the advantage of sampling many new ways of approaching experiences. The opportunity for a varied set of new experiences was supplied me in the form of moving about rather frequently. My father was a soldier for a fair portion of his life, and we lived in several places along the Eastern seaboard. In addition, he held supplementary jobs quite frequently, in order to extend the family income, and he would involve the family in many of his small financial ventures. At one time, he packaged garlic at home, and as youngsters under ten years of age, my sister and I, along with my parents, would spend many spare hours peeling and cleaning garlic cloves. Indeed, friends, neighbors and visitors would find themselves sitting in the circle, adding cleaned garlic to the large pot in the center, whenever they stopped in. At another time, we helped my father package noodles in cellophane bags. It seems safe to say that, as a family, we were quite industrious, even though the economic return somehow remained minimal. Nevertheless, the many little work experiences, and the active participation of the family broadened my perspective of the meaning and value of work, a necessary feature for a person who is to counsel with a variety of people.

My early schooling holds few active memories for me today. I was apparently a bright student, an avid reader, but essentially undisciplined in my studies. I recall running around with a gang of boys who were frequently in trouble with the school authorities, though not unduly so. School was looked upon as a necessary chore, to be tolerated until the dismissal bell.

My family was too occupied with eking out an existence, particularly during the depression years, to be much involved with my school activities, and I don't recall their doing much reading or following other more scholarly pursuits which would set examples for the children. At one period, when I was about four or five, my father attempted night school to learn drafting, but he did not sustain the effort. There is probably some significance to the fact that my parents did not attend my junior-high and senior-high-school graduations, and that I subsequently did not attend any of the ceremonies for my higher degrees.

My life goals as a boy and a teenager seemed to have some of the same element of diffusion as the rest of my activities at that time. On the one hand, I was oriented toward a humanitarian profession, that of medicine. I'm unclear about the basis for this aim, except that I was a highly empathic youngster, and found a great deal of satisfaction in helping others. On the other hand, I became strongly attracted to the notion of going to West Point. Indeed, going to the Academy was the overweening goal of my adolescence, and I was actively encouraged by my father, whose military career was of great importance to me.

He had enlisted in 1915, and was a member of Black

Jack Pershing's punitive expedition against the Mexican bandit Pancho Villa. Even at that time, he was part of the Air Corps, when it was a branch of the Signal Corps, and remained with aviation all during his military life. He retired from the service in 1945, having served actively in both World Wars, ending up as a master sergeant.

My struggle to identify and compete with my father in the process of becoming a person in my own right adds testimony to the idea already well known in the field of vocational psychology and counseling—that the goals people select have roots in their relations with the important people in their lives.

These aspirations led me to carry a college preparatory program in high school. The academic work was fairly vigorous, and I carried a full load of Mathematics, English, Science, History, and a foreign language. However, most of my closest friends avoided the academic program, and I did not win much favor because of my studies. In addition, I was resistive to the discipline of study, and devoted most of my time to competitive athletics and after-school jobs. Consequently, I took minimum advantage of my high-school experiences, as far as developing academic skills and insights was concerned.

From the time that I became professionally involved in helping young people to work out meaningful goals for themselves, I have seen this struggle to co-ordinate their goals with their ideals and their energies over and over again. However, I have found few short cuts to help resolve the diffusion of effort found at this stage in a person's life.

After high-school graduation in 1941, I was successful in competing for entrance to Queens College, but because I was young and undisciplined, my first year at college was a dismal failure. The change from constant supervision in the high-school classrooms to relative autonomy at college left me quite bewildered. My grades were poor, my adjustment to college life was equally sad, and I left after the first semester to go to work. The attack on Pearl Harbor that December gave me the excuse needed in order to save face, and I'm certain that my life today would have been vastly different had World War II not erupted at that time for the country. I probably never would have returned to college. The campus, the students, the style of life, all were quite foreign to me, and I felt almost hopelessly inadequate there.

A variety of brief experiences as a mail clerk, a messenger in a governmental agency, and a junior clerk in a supply section of the Navy, led me to look into the possibilities of developing a trade. As a result of the increase in tempo of wartime developments, I was able to apply and become accepted as a machinist's apprentice. This was an especially difficult time for me, because many of my friends were enlisting in the services, and I was found to be both color blind, and to have a scarred eardrum. I was therefore ineligible for the Navy or Marines, though I applied a number of times in different places; and being not yet eighteen, I was too young for the Army.

As with many families during the war period, mine lost its cohesiveness. My father was already overseas in Australia, my mother was working at the Brooklyn Navy Yard, my sister was in high school, and my younger brother was boarding in a military school, there being no one at home to care for him.

Circumstances, and dissatisfaction with my slow progress at the machine shop led me to drop what was left of my family life, and I went to California with a close friend, at the age of seventeen. For approximately eight months, I worked at various machine shops in and about Los Angeles, while I roomed first at a small downtown hotel, and later at the home of my friend's uncle, a Russian scholar and musician near Hollywood. My friend, Buddy, left soon afterward to become an aviation cadet in Texas. The interest and consideration his uncle, Gregory Golubeff, and his family showed me at that time was the only thing which reduced the intense loneliness I felt, living in a highly impersonal and striving environment.

My feelings of loneliness led me to become quite introspective at this time, and I began to seek out ways to understand my discontent. It was then that I discovered the field of psychology and psychiatry in the form of Menninger's book, *Love Against Hate,* and this marks the beginning of my developing a psychological point of view.

Like many people of the depression, I had come from deprived circumstances and was enjoying, superficially at least, the satisfaction of making my own living and not worrying about the financial situation. This is one of the side benefits of wartime in a culture such as ours. At the same time, youth, loneliness, and inability to find adequate self-expression, resulted in my being intensely nationalistic, even more than most, and I sought refuge in the idealistic notion that my efforts served our national cause. Consequently, I worked from twelve to fourteen hours a day, frequently seven days a week. To say that I was happy at my trade is to be charitable. At best, I was able to maintain my share of the output, but much of the time at the turret lathe involved daydreaming about the future when I would be in the Army. Indeed, I still naïvely felt that once in the Army, I could study and apply for the competitive exams and appointment to West Point through the Regular Army.

Two circumstances, occurring close together, helped to crystallize further the occupational direction I was to take later. My mother transferred to another supply depot for the Navy, this time only forty miles away from me on the West Coast. She brought with her my brother and sister, and we were together again.

At the same time, the Army announced the development of a specialized training program for young men who could qualify intellectually. They would send these men to colleges to build a pool of resources for specialized work in the service. I successfully passed the exams, but was turned down because of my scarred eardrum again, and I was in deep despair. Just around this time, my father flew in on furlough, and while visiting, succeeded in convincing the military board that my physical handicap was not sufficient to preclude my usefulness to the service, particularly if I were to be trained in some academic specialty.

I was allowed to enter the service, took an infantry basic training in Georgia, and was assigned to an engineering program at Oklahoma A & M College. This assignment plays an important part in my becoming an academician, for at Oklahoma A & M, I was able to identify with a bright and able group of young men, most of whom had previous college experience. We lived on a beautiful college campus, and there was sufficient military discipline to help me to buckle down and develop some consistency in studying. I redeemed myself academically, and for the first time felt that I belonged somewhere.

The Army specialized training program was short lived.

There was an increasing demand for combat troops; our unit at Oklahoma A & M was disbanded, and we were reassigned to infantry divisions. For the next six months, I was a member of a rifle company of the 103rd Infantry Division, in Texas. This was an extremely rigorous experience, and my athletic past stood me in good stead. In addition, I learned much of the meaning of group effort, and the extent to which the human organism is able to endure stress.

We had to learn how to co-ordinate our efforts for mutual protection and gain. Since our living conditions were primitive, and we were being trained to endure privation, feelings were frequently quite raw, and each man was confronted continually with his attitudes and values toward himself and others. Observing the interpersonal reactions of my many buddies and my own under such conditions as long, forced marches, living in dirt and mud, eating poorly for extended periods, gave me an increased sense of trust in our capacities to exist under pressure. The sense of trust and respect for another person through having lived with suffering is perhaps a basic ingredient in effective counseling, and I look upon my infantry experience as having helped to crystallize this insight in me.

Just prior to embarking for overseas, I suffered an acute appendicitis and was operated on. My outfit was gone by the time I left the hospital, and the consequence of this separation was to shape and specify my professional direction.

Post-operative cases were assigned to a reconditioning unit attached to the post hospital, where they were physically rehabilitated before reassignment to combat infantry units. While assigned to this unit, I became acquainted with the medical commanding officer, Major Robert Johnson. Prior to my operation, my company had been on an extended bivouac, and what had been a minor acne problem had become an aggravated condition. This skin problem interested Dr. Johnson, and he extended my assignment to the reconditioning unit to reduce the acne infection.

Assigned also to this unit were neuro-psychiatric patients being rehabilitated before reassignment to limited duty, or for medical discharge. I became quite absorbed in the problems of these men, their intense feelings of inadequacy, worthlessness, isolation and consequent loneliness. Curiously, most of them were intellectually competent, had come from substantial backgrounds, and were educated persons. I found myself drawn to these men, and secured a great deal of satisfaction in helping them to express their concerns and their despair.

This was noticed by Dr. Johnson, and we had many talks about the nature of these problems. That I had a flair for communicating with these men soon became evident, and Dr. Johnson managed to have me assigned temporarily to help with the rehabilitation program.

A year later, the rehabilitation unit was broken up, and I was reassigned to personnel work in the military police. My final tour of duty took place as a personnel sergeant major on board a troop transport, transferring prisoners to labor battalions in other countries, and bringing troops back to the United States. This was an experience with both personnel practices and leadership problems which undoubtedly increased my perspective in dealing with personnel concerns, though I had no clear intention then of becoming involved later on in such work.

My military experience helped to consolidate me as a person and gave me a renewed sense of confidence in my potential, and at the same time disillusioned me. Much of the arbitrariness of decisions which affected men's lives, the undue attention to status and rank, and an appalling lack of consideration for the worth of individuals had aroused my sense of injustice. This destruction of the illusions about the essential goodness and sweetness of life, and the amount of individual suffering occurring about me, combined with my own developing sense of personal adequacy, gave me a feeling of purpose and a direction in which to find self-expression.

I resolved to complete my undergraduate work in psychology and then continue on to obtain a law degree, feeling that an increased understanding of human behavior would combine with a knowledge of the law to make me more effective in helping to reduce social ills.

A refresher course at a junior college and two more in psychology at Stanford University opened my eyes to many more aspects of the daily struggle to locate oneself. Many of my fellow students were ex-servicemen who felt restless and uneasy about their new status as students. The tempo of college life seemed wrong; they weren't accomplishing their vague purposes rapidly enough. Many were married and had children, and a college program was viewed strictly as a means to an end, to be completed as soon as possible so as to get on with the real business of living.

The intensity of purpose brought by these postwar veterans made it quite difficult for the younger non-veteran and girl students. In the first place, the standards of scholarship rose sharply. In addition, these younger people seemed immature and unformed in comparison with their older classmates. They felt quite inadequate and shallow in their daily college ventures, a feature which brought an increase in the sense of diffusion on the college campus. I again found myself listening and paying attention to the problems of others, spending much of my time helping them to clarify their mixed and confused feelings about themselves.

To add to the complication of the social scene, the war years—requiring the stepping up of the tempo of exploration, invention and organization—had brought about a re-examination of many of the ideas and values which we previously took for granted. Consequently, curriculums once thought adequate had to be scrapped or revamped, textbooks had to be rewritten, all in order to meet the demands placed upon them by the magnitude and sheer quantity of new information. The teachers were thus to be considered and counted as contributing to the general ferment on the campus, and in myself. Perhaps their greatest contribution to my development at this time was their continuous challenge to examine an issue and to force me to new insights about even the most obvious. This intellectual challenge was a source of great satisfaction to me, for I was beginning to become much more independent in my approach to ideas, and needed the opportunity to roam freely in intellectual spheres, and to find out for myself the value of inquiry.

The war years and the increased specialization of military efforts also brought the college campus much closer to the rest of the world. Colleges and universities were sources of invention and exploration, and the academicians went beyond the laboratories and libraries, and into the striving business and industrial world as consultants and resource people. For one period, as a student, I assisted a professor who acted as a consultant for a market-research firm, and we interviewed consumers about their opinions and attitudes regarding peanut butter. We also had the advantage of attending invitational conferences when industrial leaders met on campus to re-examine contemporary social problems.

Thus, the college campus ceased to be an isolated community of scholars, and was brought closer to areas of reality and immediate consequences. The demands made by industrial organizations for personnel, the encouragement given by governmental and social agencies to examine vital issues of the daily social scene, further compounded the stream of variables accounting for the surge of restless searching for answers to the multitude of problems besetting the contemporary world.

The fact that the boundary lines between the college campus and the rest of the world were evaporating was of importance to me. I was still overawed by the status of the "educated man," the college professor, and I found it difficult to see myself in the company of such esteemed people. To find them dealing with mundane activities such as taking part in political activities, building their own homes, and sharing common experiences with them, made them much more human and identifiable for me.

It was in this kind of climate that my occupational plans took on even more definite form. In keeping with my desire to become socially useful, the study of psychology sensitized and brought into focus individual behavior in a social setting for me. This was particularly so because the range of my experiences in the years before going back to college needed to be placed in some form of useful and meaningful perspective.

However, I was made sharply aware that psychology as a science sought answers only to questions about behavior, and did not presume to prescribe ways to cure social ills of the world. That remained for people with ethical considerations to apply their insights about human nature in a productive manner.

At the same time, I began to find that the course of study

in Law emphasized the past traditions of logical reasoning in what seemed to me to be a painfully tight design of formal and rigid structure. As I think about it now, this resistance to form was still part of my struggle against becoming disciplined. It might be interesting to note that while I was actively resisting one form of discipline, I was apparently becoming imbued with another one, namely the scientific method. Psychology emphasized the experimental, empirical approach to the study of behavior, and its only demand was the strict adherence to the criteria of scientific methods.

But scientific effort demands a rather dispassionate approach to life if objectivity is to be optimally maintained. There still existed in me a rather strong need to see the social consequences of my efforts; and research activity, while basic to my developing philosophy, was still not a sufficient condition to determine my ultimate goal. In response to my very rewarding experiences with the rehabilitation program in the Army, clinical psychology seemed to loom increasingly on my horizon, but something kept deterring me from resolving to take that direction.

In my senior year at Stanford, I took an elective course called Introduction to Education, given by an unusually stimulating instructor who later became my friend. This course opened my eyes to the whole vista of the educational process, and put into place for me some previously unrelated variables.

I suddenly became aware that clinical efforts, for the most part, are in the nature of repair processes, *ex post facto* conditions which need treatment. Educational efforts, on the other hand, represented creative, developmental processes. The learning process, it became clearer to me, was an experimental issue of the learner at almost every step of the way, in which change occurred from one stage of readiness to another.

However, within this developmental process, I saw all about me many frustrated students and failures who were unable to gain productively from the learning situation. Tremendous amounts of energy seemed to be used up resistively, and in other misdirected ways. Not only could it be seen at the college level, but my experiences with schools through the course in Education indicated that many children in the elementary and secondary grades were striving to fulfill themselves in an unintegrated fashion. Needless to say, my own past history in high school, and my first experiences in college were seen more clearly in light of these explorations.

Further course work in Child Psychology and Adolescence, and in the psychological assessment of children and their problems, and I reached a firm decision about my professional goal. I decided to enter school psychological work, to bring to school problems a discipline involving psychological insights and methods of investigation. A year's further work in Psychology and Education to achieve a master's degree, and I was ready to enter the field.

However, I found that school superintendents were wary of young psychologists who had no experience in dealing with classroom problems. What could they know of the teacher's problems with parents and children? How could they help conflicted youngsters to adjust to the stresses of the modern school community?

Accordingly, I was offered a job in a growing school system as a school psychologist if I agreed first to put in a year in the classroom as a regular teacher. This was acceptable to me, and I taught a social-studies course called Senior Problems (there being no psychology taught at the high-school level in that school system) daily to five classes of thirty-five high-school seniors each, for a whole year.

There is no gainsaying the fact that firsthand experience introduces one to the incredibly wide range of variables affecting the success of a classroom teacher in our culture. We may talk about our experiences as students in the American high school, and argue the merits of a variety of approaches to the problem of assisting teenagers to achieve academically and socially, but until one has met with one hundred and seventy-five individuals daily from diverse value systems, motives, styles of behavior, to present them with ideas and learning materials prescribed by law, the debate must remain academic for him.

Consider, for example, the problems I encountered in a senior class examining the laws involving the police powers of a state, when the thinking capacities of the students ranged from that of an average thirteen-year-old to that of an average twenty-four-year-old; when some could read only as well as an average third-grader while others read better than average college professors; when some were completely unconcerned about anything but getting away from the strait-jacketed classroom while others were so imbued with the issues under the discussion that they monopolized class time.

To give these students a common examination upon which depended their graduation was to automatically doom some and to make others disproportionately superior. Some of the latter, who went on to the university, found to their dismay that they were merely average among college students, thereby suffering through painful disullusionment. In a number of instances, these ordinarily bright students have been handicapped in their academic development precisely because there was an unrealistic set of comparisons being made in their high-school years, and they found that it was not so necessary to maintain any consistency in study to get good grades.

I learned much from these students and from my classroom colleagues about some of the critical dynamics of a classroom learning situation. Then, as a psychologist, working with all grade levels and coming into contact with the multitude of individual problems to be dealt with in a complex school society, I was given a much clearer perspective as to the meaning of individual differences being expressed on a college campus.

Four years of daily concentration of human beings at the active developmental stage of adolescence, working with dedicated adults who were trying to balance the demands for excellence in achievement by the adult community of parents with the active ambivalence of conformity and resistance so markedly apparent in American teenagers, and I was ready to accept the invitation offered me to join the Psychology staff at San Francisco State College.

By this time, I had almost completed my work toward the doctorate with a major emphasis in counseling psychology, and I had become interested in the notion of helping embryo teachers to develop their latent abilities and skills to understand the dynamics of individuals in the learning situation.

Thus, I began my college-teaching career, having come to that position without having a clear sense of that direction, but also without any sense of regret for those experiences which led up to it. I find that many of the problems confronting the college professor demand an orientation of problem-solving such as is required of any progressive organization person, with the added advantage of being able to use the problem situation as a learning laboratory for the student.

After five years at San Francisco State College, with a sprinkling of summer-teaching experiences at several other colleges and universities in the country, I have begun to question the implications of our current approach to providing education beyond the high school for our young adults.

While a large number of students are succeeding in benefiting from their college experiences, I'm impressed by the undue proportion of those who are lost. They don't know where they are going, they hardly know why they are on campus, and they haven't found an effective use for their resources, let alone a knowledge of what these may be. The concerns expressed by these students have the same ring to them as those I heard in the high school. "I'll be glad when I get out and earn some money," they say.

As a matter of fact, I'd say that college educations are rapidly acquiring the status only recently held by the high school. That is, the symbol of educated readiness for full membership in our society, which has previously been the high-school diploma, is now being replaced by the baccalaureate. The attitudes toward being at college are likewise in transition.

In my work at the Counseling Center on campus, and in countless discussions with students in my Psychology courses, I am impressed by the number of people who express mixed feelings about being at college. I might generalize the collected impressions and paraphrase them like this: "If I were sure that the lack of a college degree would not hold me back in the future, I would not be here." The quest is not so much for knowledge about the world, or interest in some specialized field, as it is anticipating a future sense of social and economic self-enhancement. "What good will all this do me?" says the young sophomore, as he surveys his courses in

English Literature, French, Biology and Economics. "I want to be a physicist, and I don't have a single course in Physics." So he resentfully takes the above required courses and attempts to squeeze by them with a minimum of investment. Two aspects of this problem may be argued. First, the student has no perspective regarding the value of the broad educational experience at his stage in life; secondly, he may change his mind about Physics once he enters the field of courses. Further, our college faculties are dedicated to the notion that the role of the college is to develop the "well-rounded man."

I would be interested in seeing a study of the ways in which young men and women with four years of college are differentiated from a like number of people, matched for aptitude, who have had no college experience. I'm suggesting that if the two groups can be differentiated, the critical features will be nonessential ones. I'm further suggesting that the real issue is a status one.

From a status point of view, the achievement of a college degree has become almost a social necessity for a young man or woman, without which the task of proving oneself in the eyes of the community becomes a tremendously weighty one.

He may not know who he is, or what he wants to do in life, except in the broadest sense, but one thing is clear to him: he won't arrive without a degree.

I, for one, accept the idea that in our social system, a college education will be increasingly the path to full membership. This implies, of course, that many different kinds of colleges will have to emerge, in order to meet the levels of ability and the variety of skills needed to maintain our complex culture. We, at San Francisco State, in response to the needs and demands from the larger community around us and the students we attract, have been carefully building a set of curriculums consistent with what the faculty judge as vital to the various fields, but also in tune with our contemporary world. St. John's College, in Maryland, on the other hand, still maintains its Great Books program as the central part of its curriculum. The students of this small, fine, liberal arts college are very carefully selected, and probably come from a common socio-economic segment of our population. At San Francisco State, a good number of our students come from minority groups, are almost totally self-supporting, and are striving to pull away from the ghettos and the neighborhoods of the poor and the hopeless.

Obviously, there will always be a common core of material which all students will have to master if we are to maintain some sense of communality. These courses, in such a case, will include the communication skills of language and mathematics.

The many vested interests in our system will insure the perpetuation of their points of view through our educational programs, and so we will have the arts and sciences, technical and humanist societies, each fighting to achieve their fair share of the student's time and energy. In this manner, the society maintains itself, which, in the final analysis, is the reason for the existence of a college anyway.

From my point of view, the processes of the college educational program may be classified into two broad categories, each intimately dependent upon the other. On the one side of the program exist those processes and their adherents whose function it is to maintain our social system, its values, its symbols and its treasures. They keep up the standards, and insure the continuation of their conceptions of the good life. On the other side are the explorers, the rebels, the malcontents, who are not particularly satisfied with things as they are, and who encourage efforts which invite change. Individuals from both camps may be found in almost every area of study, from archeology to zoology.

I see myself in the latter group, and I am content to let my colleagues who are exasperated and frustrated by each new batch of students because of their inability to meet the standards and expectations of the "good" college student, struggle and worry over new ways to prevent dilution of the good life. I trust them to keep the rest of us in line when we wander too far afield.

My feeling is that the maintenance role of the college professor, while necessary to some degree in presenting his particular discipline, can be so subtly seductive that the so-called authority can soon come to feel that he is the keeper of Knowledge, judge and jury of the Truth, and he will soon find himself spending most of his energies criticizing others.

The greatest excitement in the learning process exists for me when discovery occurs. The student who achieves a new insight, who experiences that feeling of "aha!" and who gains one more sense of personal reward for having ventured into uncertainty, is the object of my efforts. True, I can chastise him for making mistakes, and expose his naïveté and poor judgment, and I suppose that I do this at times, but the consequence of this method of guidance of an explorer in life is to increase his dependence on the guide, and to reduce his sense of self-confidence and trust. I find that if I am able to tolerate the confusion and the ambiguity of the student's tentative explorations as we investigate an issue together, he soon arrives at his own mistakes and corrects for them without having to depend on me to change him. I realize that this type of permissive attitude does not set well by my colleagues who see themselves as hardheaded realists, and I suppose that in those areas of specific skills the coaching approach seems to be more efficient, but I'm afraid that the notion of efficiency frequently obscures the longer-range goals of self-sufficiency and independence based upon substantial criteria.

My experience leads me to believe that the tempo of change and intellectual maturity varies with individuals. Some need more time than others, and will not make up their minds about an issue until they are reasonably secure about their data. Others are more willing to risk themselves and to make many mistakes as part of their development, and I feel that they need the climate and opportunity to do so if they are to achieve any long-lasting effects of their learning experiences.

However, this is not to assume that students don't demand direction from their mentors. On the contrary, one of the most difficult jobs of the college professor, in my estimation, is to develop practices which lead to instilling in the student a sense of self-direction.

Since many students are quite unclear about their reasons for being at college, it follows that they are also unclear as to why they are in certain courses. They are frequently satisfied to assume that whatever the professor says goes, and that he must know what is good for the student, otherwise he wouldn't be presenting the material he does. Therefore, they constantly say in a variety of ways, "Tell me what I'm supposed to know." While this manifestation of dependency tends to occur more frequently at the lower levels, it may also be seen at the graduate levels. The expressions of dependency are perhaps the clearest indication to me that the attitudes toward education in the high school have transferred to the college scene.

This dependent state doesn't rest well with many of the

students I encounter. They want to be self-directing, but for many reasons—one of which is simply lack of encouragement and opportunity to experience the various aspects involved in developing self-dependence—they are unprepared. It is not simply *laissez-faire* relations they seek, as so many of our critics of youth imply. And of course, they are bound to struggle against arbitrariness of direction. Rather, I feel that they are seeking opportunities to experience for themselves the consequences of their actions, but with a more experienced individual available when he is needed.

Even then, for the more experienced person to provide the answers when the student is on the verge of his own discovery of them, is to somehow short-circuit the process of self-realization and deprive him of an experience of his own. My practice is to remain interested and encouraging, but not to accede to doing the work of exploration and the thinking for the student. Thus, it seems to me, the means of education become more consistent with the ends in mind, for we are not so much interested in providing encyclopedic information to the student as much as we hope to enable him to find out knowledge for himself. I suspect, however, that if we examine the standard procedures of educating our students on the college campus, from the point of view of desired consequences, we could easily conclude that far from encouraging independence of thought and action, we are still controlling them to a high degree.

An example of our controlling devices is the tendency to evaluate student responses as right or wrong, in a two-valued system, even though we are well aware today that few situations, ideas, or results can be relegated to such a narrow classification. We fail to clarify to the student the notion that evaluation is ultimately a question of judgment and compromise, and these are matters of equity. In my own case as a teacher, one of my minor goals is the achievement of a sense of equity in the evaluation process in all aspects of life.

Evaluation is a constant consideration in an achievement-oriented culture such as ours, and I habitually exploit its existence in my classes as an object lesson in identifying the essentially compromising features of evaluation. Several advantages immediately accrue for me as the teacher. In spending a portion of the time with my classes exploring the question of how we shall evaluate the course experiences, the efforts and contributions of its members, the students are forced to examine why they are in the class, what they expect to achieve from it, what kinds of efforts should receive credit, and how we can make the learning experience meaningful to the greatest number of students.

It is always a source of reassurance to me that, when students are given the opportunity to explore this aspect of their learning experience, they become highly involved with their own learning, and rarely evade committing themselves to more effort than I would expect. Furthermore, the process of realistic compromise receives a careful and thorough examination, and the student learns the meaning of arbitration in the face of a wide range of differences in standards, values and orientations.

Still another procedure I use in order to facilitate the regime of self-appropriated learning is to have the students participate in the development of the agenda of the course. I have found that people are motivated to learn about those issues which have meaning and value to them. When these students sit down in small groups to thrash out together the things they expect to learn from their experiences in my class, I find that their agenda approximates to a high degree the course outline I would have suggested. Their terms may differ from mine, but their questions and ideas are operationally appropriate. In addition, their agenda usually compares quite favorably with course contents found in texts for the particular classes.

The major difference is that the course-content goals emanate from the students and are their property, and have not been handed down to them from the authority figure. This removes some of the basic resistance found in students who are pulling away from authority figures in their lives anyway, and they are encouraged thereby to test out their own inclinations. This slight, but major, distinction is vital to the other aspects of my course procedures, for I feel that if the student is to function consistently with his own meaningful purposes, he first has to become aware of them to the extent that he can find direction from them. What follows is an increased availability to participate in all phases of his learning experiences.

It is probably apparent by this time, that my inclination is to develop instructional practices which work at the intimate, face-to-face level, and which require active participation by the broadest number of students. However, my own passion for examining various aspects of human interaction led me to participate in an experiment involving instruction via television.

The college received some two hundred thousand dollars from the Ford Foundation to study the effects of televised instruction when compared with conventional classroom instruction. My part in this study was to present thirty forty-five minute telecasts of a course entitled Psychology of Personal and Social Development to freshman students who would view the course at home through their own television sets. They were to be compared with a matched group of students who took the same course on the campus with me. Both groups were studied for changes in attitudes, achievement, general course information and relations with fellow students.

Briefly, the results were comparable to similar studies undertaken at other college and university campuses. Both groups benefited significantly from the courses, and there were no differences found between them, other than in the area of relations with fellow students. Each member of my campus class of thirty-five students got to know every other student in the class, and achieved binding friendships, while few of the students taking the course at home via television got to know each other.

From the instructional point of view, I must confess that learning to televise a set of experiences from which the student could gain meaningful insights into his own behavior, and that of others about him, was a painful process for me. My whole prior orientation to sound learning was the active participation of students in their own learning experiences, and at firsthand, if possible. Conducting a class via television required my shifting over to traditional practices in almost every respect. The learner was forced to be passive, and was unable to stop me when he became confused, or needed to seek clarification, or wanted to add an additional point. I, in turn, was forced to direct almost wholly the thinking of the student, without knowing if I was communicating, or was proceeding too rapidly or too slowly.

I found, however, that if I could design little dramatic vignettes, in which the characters were portrayed by drama students, the viewing student could take from the experience portrayed that which was meaningful to him. In this manner,

I was able to provide some approximation of reality experiences for the learner, and I could talk on the issues and controversies pointed up in the dramatic scenes.

Talking about experience without having first experienced is for me a very unsatisfying procedure. The alternatives are only illusion and analogy, and these can only go so far toward clarifying reality.

Providing the student an opportunity to deal with his notions of reality in a productive and meaningful way has come to be my central focus as a college professor. Part of a student's struggle with reality is his slow emergence from childlike dependency to a sense of mature perspective about himself and the world around him. This perspective is constantly enlarging for all of us who seek to know things. I would describe this as the educational process, in which all of a student's experiences, in school and out, are grist for his mill. If he is to gain from his experiences, he has to learn to view them from a countless number of positions. This requires a sense of freedom to shift from one position to another, to make errors of perception and judgment, to return and re-examine, to question himself, and everyone else, if he must.

My task is to indicate my trust and support, and encouragement of him and his capacity as an ethical, thinking person in his own right, to reach whatever conclusions are meaningful to him in the light of his data and experience, and my satisfactions lie in the opportunity to accompany him in his venture.

San Francisco State College

. . . A Conservative View

GLENN LEGGETT

I WAS reared in a middle-sized town on Lake Erie, in northeastern Ohio. My parents had lived there from childhood; their own parents had lived and worked respectably there, and all of us were easy and comfortable in it. I was born in the house my grandfather had built, and so were all my brothers and my sister. My mother, who was a registered nurse and ministered to her children and to the neighbors at the merest whimper, had a sure instinct for knowing what ailed people, no squeamishness at all in handling the sick or injured, and a crusading scorn for what she called the "impersonal inefficiency" of most doctors and all hospitals. When her own parents became permanent invalids, she moved them into our house and nursed them herself, over the objections of her relatives and the quiet wonder of my father. She was a beautiful tyrant herself, demanding both absolute power and absolute love, and at least in my youthful eyes, getting both. Her will was like that of a child, naked and limitless, and managed by a set of reflexes so fast that I do not remember any circumstance or personality catching her off guard. Her talents for supervision were enormous, and she ran a closely regulated household: things were always in their places, and eating and dishwashing and going-to-bed were performed on schedule. But I do not remember being unhappy with this orderliness, partly because the hand that inspired it, though quick and sure, was not heavy, and partly because the whole family contributed to it, quite naturally and without fussing. In later years when I learned about the psychopathology of too much orderliness, I was only momentarily embarrassed about what it suggested about my own personality. A belief in system and organization was so ingrained in me that the absence of them seemed almost a moral evil; indeed, most of my attempts to be reasonable about myself have been similarly futile, and I trace the failure to an early conditioning by my mother.

I was the eldest of five children, four sons and a daughter. One brother died in infancy and is only a picture in a photo album, but another, the youngest of all, died just short of his teens while I was in college. As I look back, it was his dying that fixed a depression on my parents they never recovered from, and made me slightly, but permanently, distrustful of life. Yet at the time, after the first terrible weeks, I thought we were all taking the experience in stride. We were, at any rate, a relaxed and easygoing family, with dozens of relatives and friends constantly and casually walking in and out of the front and back doors, or staying to eat and visit, with no skeletons in any closet that I ever heard of or suspected, and if there was not plenty of money, there was enough so that no one worried about it. I do not remember my parents ever arguing seriously. My mother had too much of a temper to do it well, and my father was too gentle to do it at all. Indeed, when, as a typical graduate student, I read Freud and tried to get my mother and father into the melodrama of my own id, I never had any luck giving them villainous parts to play. They were extraordinarily good people and they performed so efficiently as parents that only recently have I realized how much uncertainty lay beneath my mother's positive competence and how many irritations were covered by my father's gracious manner of being imposed upon.

My father was the editor of the town's newspaper. My mother's brother was the city manager. I grew up with the feeling that everybody knew me, and I probably made capital of the fact, but there were enough people in town who disliked the newspaper and the city administration to teach me the virtues of modesty. I never had any doubt then, nor do I now, that both my father and uncle were on the right side, but there was a short time in college when I thought all conservatives were either secret agents or well-intentioned dupes of something called Wall Street and found the premises of my logic forcing me to believe that my father and uncle were either crooked or ignorant. But the fact that they were neither wore out the logic quickly, and I gave up philosophic systems that insisted on "either-or" belief. Abstractions and generalizations made me uncomfortable; they were always being bombarded with exceptions, either in the form of situations or people, and though I had my mother's capacity for ignoring what didn't fit the wish, I lacked her emotional courage for justifying and building on it, so that what has resulted for me, as an administrator, is a manner of energetic improvisation, of intuitive system and purpose, sometimes at the expense of articulated theory or plan.

Neither of my parents was an intellectual, or even academically inclined, though my father read widely and read well. Not being a college graduate himself, he had an inordinate respect for those who were, and he always assumed that I would go to college. But I do not recall hearing from him any of the regular clichés about what a college education was supposed to do for me: no talk about its improving the family social position or standard of living. From what I could see, these were satisfactory enough. And he was too hardheaded to be misled by a promise of "finer things in life" for me. A college education will give you understanding, he would say; but he never volunteered any details and I never knew the questions to ask to get them. My mother would say to me privately that it was too bad my father had not had a college education—he would have known how to use it. And then she would make a scornful remark about one of his contemporaries who had been to college but had learned nothing. But whatever my father's ingenuousness about the benefits of a college education, he was truly professional about his own work. In my limited experience, he was one of the most competent newspapermen I've ever known. In those days, disasters and major elections were invariably reported in extra editions, usually in the middle of the night or very early in the morning, and my father's excitement and skill in helping to get them ready for the newsboys had a pervasive energy about them that raised the whole family to a marvelous fervor of organization. He used to stand at the end of the huge press, just as the foreman turned the switch that put the great rolls of paper in motion, and reach for the first copy as it came out on the conveyor. In a moment or two, after an expert glance at it, he would signal the foreman to speed up the press or, if a change were necessary, to stop it completely. When the looks of the paper satisfied him, he would walk to the loading platform and supervise the distribution of papers to vendors and newsboys, all of whom he knew by name. I was enormously proud to be his son.

As a newspaperman, however, his real virtue was a less

spectacular one, and I came to know it much later, too late in fact, for he was ill then and beyond reach of praise. He was a superb writer of exposition. He had a sure touch with editorials and human-interest stories; they were always uncluttered and focused, with the language never interfering with the material or outrunning it. He wrote them either in a crowded office, with telephones and voices jangling all around him, or in the den at home, a mere extension of the dining room, on an old L. C. Smith that took a two-fingered beating for years without breaking down. In those days, when I thought I was something of a writer myself, I'd tease him about his unmelodramatic and detached style. Compared with my own lush prettiness, it seemed almost transparent, and I used to complain that one was hardly aware of the language of his writing. Depending on his mood, he would admit, yes, it was rather dull stuff, or would ask me to read some more books and then talk with him about it. He never did talk with me about it really, but in a way it wasn't necessary. After I had read my first thousand freshman themes I knew what, in his oblique way, he had been getting at, and though my own writing would have dissatisfied him, we would have agreed on most of the reasons for its failure.

He tried, not too rigorously, to turn me into a newspaperman, with part-time and summer jobs in the newswriting offices; but while I never disliked the work, I never found myself really engaged by it. He never fussed with me about it, was adamant only about my working at something after school and in the summers. I never minded this sort of pressure; my expenses were always outrunning my allowance and I welcomed the chance to make money on my own. I remember occasional and penetrating queries about where I was spending my money, but I was never really pushed hard for answers. I never had them anyway, nor do I have them now.

I had all my pre-college training in public schools. Until my last years in high school, I was a good student. I was consistently on the honor rolls, and I remember winning two or three prizes in essay contests and in Latin examinations. I don't recall studying much, but I did read a great deal. The house was full of books, sets of Dickens, Hugo and Richard Harding Davis, and I read most of them, along with the juveniles that my generation read: Tom Swift, Poppy Ott, Tarzan and something called the Pony Rider boys. In my junior and senior years, my scholarship decayed radically. I was unfocused, given alternately to spells of profound lassitude and frenetic activity. I was constantly preoccupied with something other than what I was doing at the moment. Luckily, the momentum I'd established earlier, and the good nature of my teachers, carried me through to graduation. But one thing is certain: at that age I was no academic, and when I compare my early attitude with that of a number of my colleagues, many of whom appear to have been pre-puberty intellectuals, I am disturbed by the reasons for my own failure to be one, and sometimes given over to suspecting that if I were not an academic executive I would not be an academic at all.

With my parents' insistence that I go to college it was easy to agree, not because I had any real faith in what a college education would do for me, but because this was a way of pleasing them. It never occurred to me that they would have to give up something to send me to college, that I was in any sense using them. I was in love, for the first time, and unable to think of anything consistently but the joy and agony of it; the rest of my life was happening to somebody else. When I went away to Middlebury College in Vermont,

I had no notion of what career I wanted to prepare myself for, only that I knew I did not want to be a newspaperman and that I lacked the talent and interest to be an engineer or a doctor or a salesman, or anything really practical—something vocationally solid and question-stopping for those aunts and uncles and other interested onlookers who wanted to know, and deserved to know, what I was going to do upon graduation. But it did take me only a few terms at college to discover that I was most at home in courses which centered on understanding and using language—literature, history, economics, sociology and so forth. Because this center was wider and more pervasive in literature than in any of the others, I became an English major, still not sure I wanted to become a teacher but content for the moment to work in the vineyard, studying literature and rhetoric and becoming more and more engaged by the effect on language of human personality and intelligence.

As I look back and try to get things isolated and categorized, I think my interest in rhetoric was focused for me by a freshman-literature instructor who almost persuaded me that an understanding of words was central to an understanding of myself. I spent the rest of my undergraduate career alternately escaping and strengthening this persuasion, and though I enjoyed the difficult but tidy two-dimensional world of scientific courses, I found myself getting more and more committed to the slippery, three-dimensional world of rhetorical and literary studies, chiefly because the human personality was always at the center of it, qualifying and confusing my understanding, but enriching it, too. During these years my responses to literature were impressionistic and I suppose sentimental, almost apologetic, for I was embarrassed by an interest that might be interpreted as self-indulgent, even unmanly. It was not until later that I began to see in the structure and texture of language a way of knowing the world that made other ways appear partial or irrelevant or even inaccurate. Certainly I know now, after years of trying to find a more socially acceptable reason for my interest in rhetoric, that I became a teacher of it simply because I wanted to continue studying it.

I was a B student in college, more accurately a B minus. I kidded myself that being a fraternity man, a campus politician, and a varsity debater made exacting academic work unnecessary. But only the debating was really worth while, and that partly because it taught me something about organizing a piece of exposition and partly because the faculty debating coach, an English professor, was a remarkably perceptive and able teacher, with a profound knowledge of the self-deceptions that human beings are capable of but not the slightest desire to use it to his own advantage. He shut off completely whatever half-conscious Napoleonic urgings I had, and his own uncorroded psyche persuaded me that generosity toward other people might be frequently foolish but never sinful, not even regrettable. My other undergraduate teachers, especially those in literature, were always adequate, and sometimes exciting. As my memory watches them perform in the classroom, I see now that the best ones kept the text of the poem or play or document always before the class, shoving it forward imperceptibly with questions and comments that made us look hard through ourselves at it. The others either patronized the text wittily, or used it as a springboard to sermonize us on their own political or social or personal beliefs. They were preachers, not teachers, but some of them were so marvelously eloquent and personable that they had a whole generation of students singing their praises, and

I remember them today, not for what they taught me but for what they were.

During the summers after my freshman and sophomore years, I stayed in Vermont and worked as a waiter and bus boy at the Breadloaf Summer School and Writers' Conference. The students were mostly high-school English teachers and writers trying to get out of amateur standing, the instructors and lecturers mostly New England college professors and professional writers. The atmosphere was relaxed but stimulating, and my duties not very onerous. Though I took one course during my first year, a delightfully taught "modern poetry" by Donald Davidson, I was not really a member of the student body. I was one of a couple of dozen college-boy employees, and at the time considered myself an objective observer of the academic environment provided by the regular students and the regular teaching staff. They were probably all quite decent people, but the discrepancy between their expected and real actions shocked me at first. I had expected an idealistic behavior from those engaged in literary endeavors and found instead that they acted much like other people; indeed, that their articulateness, ironically, sometimes made them seem less, not more, attractive. It was difficult to unstuff myself, perhaps because as a waiter I was constantly being re-disillusioned about human beings in general and academics in particular: the little vulgarities, vanities and ill-manners of people dining are inevitably caricatured in the eyes of a waiter, who is ubiquitous but unnoticed and detached. The intensity of the disillusionment faded in time, and I learned not to associate it specifically with academics, but to this day I am self-conscious and overly well-mannered in the presence of a waiter, or indeed to some extent with anyone who is forced by circumstances or a system to take orders or directions from me. This attitude, though admirable in some ways, complicates my administrative life considerably, for I tend to lose the offensive to some people at the very moment I should be exercising it most vigorously.

I gave the commencement oration at my graduation in 1940. It was about the approaching war, youth, the failure of the older generation, and the other things that young people are so sure of. In spite of its manly assertions, it reads now like a long exercise in self-pity. We would go to war, pull the older generation's chestnuts out of the fire, and magnanimously forgive them after we returned, maimed, suffering and lost in a world we never made. But in the meantime, between graduation and the draft board, there was a career to get started. I returned to Ohio, mostly concerned with guessing how soon I would be in the army, wishing betimes that something or somebody would make a definite decision about my future. My parents' response to this situation was typical and quick, that I might as well work at something useful until I reached a decision or until one was reached for me. My father helped get me a job with the power and light utility in Cleveland, Ohio, and there I spent the summer, living with a bachelor friend in a small apartment, and working as a kind of secretary-receptionist to one of the sales managers. It was a time-clock job, eight to five, eighty dollars a month. My working routine was to answer the phone politely, write business letters, and keep track of the salesmen as they called in periodically from their allotted districts in the city. The duties were not unpleasant, and indeed, once students are substituted for salesmen, very much like part of the administrative housekeeping I do now. But it was a dead end, for the best positions in the company were designed for electrical engineers or super-salesmen, and

I knew I could be neither. Yet my real decision to leave at the end of the summer did not rest on a concern for my future earning power. The company certainly performed useful services, and its bosses were considerate and humane; but neither my imagination nor energies were captured by the prospect of staying there. It was a kind of laziness on my part, I told myself, a damnable indirection and lack of adult discipline, but I wanted to get back in an academic environment and be a student again. My father looked at me long and hard when I told him, but he said sure and offered to pay part of my expenses.

Early that September I drove down to Columbus, Ohio, and enrolled in the Department of English as a graduate student. I rented a single room in a private residence close to the university, got a part-time job as a waiter in a campus restaurant for my meals, and for the rest of the year did little else but go to classes, study, prowl the library, and measure myself against the other graduate students in the department. Except for the normal stresses and strains of life, I was happier than I had ever been. I knew I was irrevocably committed to rhetorical and literary studies, and I enjoyed giving all my energies to scholarship. I was full of admiration for all my professors; I listened attentively, read their publications, followed their directions meticulously. My only uneasiness came when I wondered how long, if ever, it would be before I could make a decent living doing what they were doing. When another graduate student complained about the inadequacies of some of them, I was silent; they all seemed paragons of industry and organized purpose to me. How much of this natural acceptance of authority was my ingenuousness and how much my training I do not know. It has persisted somewhat, and probably made me something of a "company man," a term that should bother me more than it does, but it is perhaps compensated for by my instinctive assumption that everyone else hates authority and should be treated gently.

During my first year of graduate study, I took three five-hour courses each quarter, wrote my thesis in the spring quarter, and had my M.A. degree in June. Though my studies in the beginning were largely in general areas and in refinements of my undergraduate training, I began to have special interests in English linguistics, and in seventeenth-, eighteenth- and twentieth-century literatures. My ambition was to prepare myself to teach these courses in any reputable institution that would hire me. I knew this meant eventually a Ph.D. degree, and I saw no reason not to begin immediately. My draft number had not come up and, other than finding a way to support myself, I thought I had nothing to detain me. When I think of how the war and no job surely complicated my security then, I am puzzled by what must have been my calm detachment; and I am almost unnerved by my own history when I recall that one week after receiving my M.A., penniless, and with no prospects of a job, I married my high-school sweetheart, one day after she had graduated from college, also penniless, with no prospects of a job. Yet twenty years later, after four children, two mortgages, an unending succession of bills and minor crises, I am grateful for the good things that innocence and ignorance of the world apparently can sometimes lead to.

After a short honeymoon, we set up housekeeping in a basement apartment, and I used my mother's influence as a Republican precinct committee woman to get a night job as janitor in the Bureau of Unemployment Compensation. I worked from four in the afternoon until midnight, sweeping and waxing floors, polishing desks and emptying wastebaskets. My colleagues were mostly middle-aged Negroes and college athletes. The former organized the work and did most of it; the latter were paid more than the rest of us, and appeared only half the time. But they were good fellows and gracious about their advantage, and I don't recall that the rest of us minded much. We were all essentially undeserving, and so naturally democratic. During the day I took a full schedule of graduate classes. Two of my instructors were visiting professors: George Boas of Johns Hopkins and Earl Leslie Griggs of Pennsylvania. They were both learned and sophisticated, and their example helped persuade me that an academic profession was the right choice for me. Their courses were seminars, the first I had taken as a graduate student: the others had been conducted as regular classes, in orthodox classrooms, with the professor lecturing or leading the discussion from behind or in front of his desk. It was in one of these seminars that the intensely competitive atmosphere of professional academic life was first emphasized to me. I had been introduced to it mildly before, in conversations and hallway gatherings with other graduate students. It seemed good-natured then, hardly worth fretting about. But in the seminar the competition was tight and articulate and personal; papers were read aloud, and criticisms directed to the author by the students through the instructor, it is true, but only made more embarrassing by the latter's attempt to rephrase them graciously. I was not much good at either the give or take of this arrangement: too sentimental to humiliate the weak and too cowardly to abuse the strong. I had developed no real critical theory to help orient and support me, and I was still naïve enough to think I should understand a critical terminology before using it. So I took refuge in playing the gentleman.

About halfway through the summer, I was told by the department chairman that I could have a teaching fellowship for the next school year if I wanted it. Though it meant a cut in my income from one hundred dollars a month to fifty, I could not deny myself the opportunity to begin teaching, even if it were Freshman English. I was now a member of the inner group of graduate students, those marked by the graduate professors as students whose promise deserved a subsidy. I was elated. I was completely unaware of the real responsibilities in teaching a subject like Freshman English, assuming only that it was a reward for graduate work well done, that it would help pay for my future training, that it would give me a chance to work off some exhibitionist tendencies before freshmen, and above all, that it would be easy. All the assumptions were true except the last one; while I had all sorts of ideas about how good communication got to be literature, I had no notion at all of how to get freshmen to put the loose junk of language into plain, literate communication. This ignorance I refused to face up to in the beginning, finding fault with the high-school training of students, with their casual attitude toward education in general, and with the whole idea of public education—to which, I suspect, I considered myself a shining exception. Apparently I had enough conscience to want to do well what I was paid to do, and as the exigencies of freshman teaching began to educate me, I saw that language and communication and literature were all of a piece: that the grammatical and rhetorical devices which turned quasi-literate into literate expression differed only in degree from those devices that turned communication into literature; that the complexities of the latter were in one sense the simplicities for the former many times compounded.

At the end of the school year, which was my second as a graduate student, I was offered a position as instructor in English and History and coach of debating at the Massachusetts Institute of Technology, at a salary of two thousand dollars. It seemed like half the money in the world. We had been living on fifty dollars a month, sharing a rented house with another graduate-student couple and their child, and though the experience was pleasant, thanks to mutually good dispositions, it was time to move on. Our first-born was expected in a few months, and the period of irresponsible self-sufficiency was coming to an end. We packed our belongings in innumerable cardboard boxes, checked them through to Boston on our railroad tickets, and departed.

We arrived early one hot afternoon in September, and walked the streets of Back Bay until we found an apartment; in a few days I went to work teaching courses in freshman composition, American Civilization and argumentation. The department was friendly, the students remarkably well-trained and educable, and in some ways I think I did the best teaching I've ever done. Though I was only an instructor, it was fun being a regular staff member, to sit in on departmental meetings, and to look upon the others as my colleagues. They were all very generous in their attitudes toward me, and three or four of them made particular efforts to train me as a teacher; they talked over my lesson plans with me, provided me with illustrations and advice, and did it all very graciously, almost fondly. Their own dedication to teaching was profound. They prepared for class meticulously, worried over their presentations, and were constantly seeking for ways to make classroom discussion more pointed and focused. Their attitude toward teaching and their eagerness to help a greenhorn impress me still, and I hope are the foundations of my own work as a supervisor of young and unexperienced teachers.

I stayed at M.I.T. two years, the last being devoted almost exclusively to teaching composition courses to students in the Navy V-12 and Army Students' Training programs. By now the pressures, mostly internal, of being a young civilian in a world of uniforms were getting too uncomfortable. I had earlier applied for a commission in the Navy and had been turned down: color perception too imperfect. I wrote my local draft board in Ohio and told them I wished to enlist. Within a month my wife and daughter were living with my parents and I was in recruit training at the Great Lakes Naval Training Center. After that I was assigned as a yeoman to the Recruit Training Command and eventually to the central office of the Center. I never set foot on a ship, was never fired upon, was never physically uncomfortable. I was busy enough during the daytime trying to master Navy clerical routine not to be bored, but the evenings and weekends were something of a problem. I think I read almost every book in the base library, from everything by Agatha Christie to everything in a late nineteenth-century edition of Sir Walter Scott. I even wrote a couple of short stories, both of which so clearly had no narrative merit that I dropped them in the wastebasket without even a melodramatic gesture.

Just a few weeks before I had enough points to be discharged. I wrote to the chairman at Ohio State and asked him if I could have back my old teaching fellowship. My plans were to use my G.I. educational subsidy to finish my graduate work as quickly as part-time teaching would allow and then find a position in a department which, after requiring the usual stint of freshman teaching from me, would make me its seventeenth- or eighteenth-century specialist. I had no desire to escape Freshman English; I had learned how important it was to my students and to my own character as a teacher. On the other hand, though my feelings toward it were warm, they were by no means overpowering, and I never thought of it as a career in itself. But instead of a fellowship, I got a full-time instructorship—enrollment was booming—and I soon found that freshmen were taking as much of my time as my graduate work. I tried at first to recapture the atmosphere of my earlier days as a graduate student. But my friends who had remained at Ohio State while I was at M.I.T. and in the service had either left or were leaving with their degrees. Poverty and innocence no longer linked the graduate students. Instructorships were to be had almost for the asking, wives could work at good salaries, the war had given everyone at least the façade of experience. Something else had changed, too: the comfortable tradition of historical scholarship that had seemed unshakeable when I'd left in 1942 was getting pushed around, and vociferously so, by a very articulate group of contemporary critics. Luckily, my informal introduction to them was through an older colleague with as much common sense as he had regard for them. My first formal introduction to them came through a graduate professor who, in teaching a seminar in seventeenth-century prose, handled the materials of recent criticism and traditional scholarship with such a quiet but sharp competence that he made them seem all of a piece, the one as necessary as the other, provided the critic was responding to a piece of literature as a disciplined, whole man and not as a neurosis on the defensive.

My own teaching during my first couple of years after returning to Ohio State was mostly in Freshman English, and because I shared an office with the assistant director, I began to get involved in the operation of the program. I was asked to interview students, work on syllabi, talk to publishers' representatives about textbooks, and help out in other ways. It was inevitable that I came to be considered the second assistant. I liked this administrative work, minor as it was: it satisfied a part of my ego that teaching and graduate work by themselves did not, and I revered the director of the program. He had the shy, hesitant manners of a country boy, the superficial disorganization of a child, but the perceptions of a poet who is also a wise old grandfather. He managed the program by personal force alone, needing almost no administrative machinery he couldn't invent at the moment and discard when it had served its purpose. Four days a week he was surely the worst administrator I have ever seen: he ignored problems that seemed to me to be screaming for attention; on the fifth day, after a series of short conversations with various members of the staff and a walk or two through the composition offices, he would eliminate almost every problem, call me into his office, tease me into inventing a few more administrative problems, and solve them on the spot. He did this affectionately, but directly, and I soon got the point. Our function is to get a group of students before an instructor so that learning can take place, he would say, and he would add that it doesn't take place in a chart of organization or in the mimeographing room. The philosophy of his approach to administration was undoubtedly oversimplified; it left some areas of persisting confusion to unnerve the staff, but I learned to accept its basic assumption that an academic administrator's sense of tidiness and control are not really of first importance.

Within a year or so the assistant director had his Ph.D.

degree and left to run a freshman composition program at another college. About the same time, the director became ill and the task of managing his program fell to me; when he returned, still ailing, I found myself his formal assistant, his "associate" as he called it. Though my interest in literary studies had not failed, I put less and less time into them, and when I did take my degree in the winter of 1949, I knew I had not tried myself out intellectually. The continuing and unrelieved pressures of teaching and administrative responsibilities, and a growing family, had taken energies that I had intended to give to hard and creative study and to discovering what, as a serious student, I could and could not do. I kept persuading myself that my original intentions had not changed, that they were only being deferred until I had mastered the details of the administrative work then taking such large chunks of my time. What happened, however, in the following years, was not less but more administrative responsibility, the result of my own decision to be sure, but perhaps predetermined once I had allowed myself to drift into an occupation whose chief function appears to be that of protecting other people from the academic housekeeping that interferes with their effective teaching and study. I suspect that the cry of an administrator is not really "Who am I?" but "What am I doing here?" and the answer to the second question doesn't encourage him to ask the first.

When I became an assistant director of Freshman English, I began to think seriously of the rationale and purposes of the program. Up until that point I had assumed it was a fixed, unvaried function, not to be thought about really, just performed. I read the literature, studied the textbooks, went to meetings, conferred with teachers. Almost at once I found the chief weakness of most Freshman English programs to lie in a temptation of their directors to isolate their problems and to study nothing else. At best the result seemed to be a program without enough context to support it; at worst a kind of special pleading and educational fixation that ended chiefly in self-justification for the program. My conviction grew that while Freshman English directors ought to know the machinery of their programs, they need principally to get respect for themselves as teacher-scholars and give their own literacy a character and a purpose. I was appalled by the number of directors who had forgotten or never realized what seemed to me the self-evidence of this fact. They had turned their programs into courses in speaking, listening, semantics, logic, psychology, social thought and even human relations. I could see that all these matters were related to the problem of teaching freshmen to write, but they seemed a bit peripheral to the job of dignifying the grounds and purposes of plain literacy, and I came to believe that the manner in which this job is executed and given direction is the Freshman English director's real importance to his university. Otherwise, he is simply isolating and advertising the grounds of his own administration existence.

What all this came to on my part is the belief that the rationale of Freshman English, to put it plainly, is to teach what is called, but isn't, simple expository writing to all kinds of recent high-school graduates who are known technically as college freshmen; that it is necessary to do this because most (but not all) high-school graduates do not write as well as they should after some twelve years of more or less formal practice in using their native tongue; and that fixing the blame for this situation, though always a fascinating exercise, has to be responsible and constructive if it is to be educationally useful. It had seemed to me that most critics, unfortunately, split into two neat groups: those who blame everything on the pervasive philosophy of John Dewey, and those who pick on the backsliding of someone like Miss Tillie Whistlesides, teacher of sixth-grade English, who talked about the latest movie when she should have talked about nouns and verbs. Both reasons have their validity, but they fall into the extremes of the overly general or the overly specific. From one point of view, though hardly a helpful one, obviously a good many things have created the situation—students, parents, taxpayers, the school system, colleges and teachers themselves: students, because they have the notion they're entitled to an education that's painless; parents, because they're so busy trying to make a living that they half-accept the point of view of their children in order to get peace in their own households; taxpayers, because they think they're the only people who really earn their money (all others being merely lucky or parasitic) and so justify their cut-the-budget complex; the school system, because it takes the people listed above too seriously; the colleges, because they often give the impression of wanting nothing to do with the secondary schools except to complain about them; and the teachers themselves, because it is their unfortunate nature to suffer fools gladly, whether they be in their own ranks or in the classroom or only in the general neighborhood making noises.

But ultimately, though, the real reason for the failure of most high-school graduates to write as well as they should is really something else: it is a general misunderstanding of what is involved in writing decently and clearly and what it takes to get a human being to do it. The public at large, as well as more schoolteachers than I care to count, look upon the process of writing as a task somewhat similar to the one a garage mechanic faces in reassembling an automobile engine. There is first the job of seeing that all necessary parts are on hand (in writing, these are thought to be the equivalent of "ideas"); then of seeing that all parts are clearly labeled, at least in the mind (these are "words," and the dictionary has a large supply if you need more); then of seeing that you have the proper tools (this is merely "grammar" or "punctuation"; either you have it or you don't, and if you don't you can borrow it or make something else do); then of seeing that the parts go in right order ("sentences") and are properly connected ("paragraphs"); then of simply stepping on the starter and driving off (final sentence and happy conclusion). Nothing could be further from the truth, and it is the unglamorous but none the less essential aim of a Freshman English course to point this out. In the first place, "ideas" are not things having an existence independent of words themselves, and it is people who think they have and say such things as "If I could only find the words to express the ideas I have" who have put the permanent crease in the English teacher's forehead. Until an idea exists in the form of words that say something, it isn't an idea at all, but a mere grunt in the mind. In the second place, in the process of writing itself, grammar and punctuation and sentences and so forth are not separately packageable items, like carburetors and spark plugs and such. Before and after writing, they can be discussed as things apart, but once the writing itself begins, they need to lose their separate identity and work together nicely, like the ingredients in a good soup: if they don't, the result is not writing but a kind of lumpy or watery hash, indigestible to all but the cook himself (and even he may have his doubts about it). Finally, and most important of all, writing clearly demands so much from the thinking, sorting and focusing powers of the human mind that it's inseparable from getting educated in general. It's no wonder that most people want to believe it's something else and unconsciously put pressure on their educational representatives to operate on the basis that it's only a matter of memory or exhortation or "creative self-expression."

Unfortunately this pressure is applied with some success, and the results are unhappy. Most teachers of English (and I do not exclude the ones in the public schools) know that the only way to teach students to write is to have them write and rewrite, constantly, under sharp and corrective supervision, with time out only for some close reading to illustrate techniques, suggest new ideas and test some old ones. The same teachers would probably agree that the sooner the student is subjected to this regimen in his academic life the better. Writing clearly and well is a skill that needs some growing up to, but writing with a decent respect for the literate amenities is largely a habit, and a habit formed early is likely to stick. (And "early" is not the second semester of senior high school; it is too late then to start a series of good habits—the old ones are almost fixed, and an eighteen-year-old cannot be flushed out like a radiator and refilled easily with sweet, clean virtues.)

But the kind of supervised practice in composition which creates good habits is expensive and time-consuming, and not very glamorous, and it is easier to talk around and about composition than to teach it directly. The result is that most high-school courses in English tend to emphasize the urge to expression, not the necessary techniques of writing, so that when a high-school graduate begins his career in Freshman English he takes, what is to him, a decidedly unfair placement examination in English. Like a lamb in the stockyards, he is then led to a proper corral and told that he is "normal," or "remedial," or "advanced." What follows for him is practice in expository writing: a paper a week, correction, revision, re-correction, another paper, and so on, week after week. His instructors seldom make an attempt to amuse or caress him; are rarely interested in what he "meant" to say but only in what he said and how he said it; do not appear to care whether he is a young fellow working every night to support his aged parents; and use the term "well-rounded personality" the way a farmer uses a mouthful of sour tobacco juice, merely to test the reflexes of everything alive that moves around him.

Most of this is an overstatement; a teacher of Freshman English is almost as human as anyone else: circumstances have just given him more than the normal number of disguises, and he should not be judged too harshly. For one thing, he is trying to get students through a writing program that ideally they should have been put through years before, and he now suspects that it is too late. For another, he knows he teaches a "service" course: he is merely getting students ready for something else—to write decent essay examinations for the political science and economics professor; to spell well enough so that law-school professors will not go quietly mad reading student briefs; to write term papers in special fields that will be models of directness, documentation and intelligibility; and in general to think lucidly on paper no matter for whom. He is rather sure that only a few of his students will do all these things properly. Some of the rest will blame their failure on him; and his colleagues in other departments, without saying a word, will give him the same impression. But other students will return one day, at least in spirit, to thank him for refusing to side-step his commitment that "plain and simple writing" describes an end product only. The method is anything but that—hard, somewhat uninspiring and occasionally downright uncomfortable. The rationale of Freshman English is this method, and one of the tasks of a director is to persuade his colleagues and the public at large that the method is both necessary and honorable.

These were my convictions when I came to the University of Washington in 1952 as director of Freshman English, and they remain. I found that the department chairman and my predecessor had them, too; and that the program I inherited was tight and sensible, and the staff disciplined and professional. The department as a whole, however, did not seem sufficiently engaged by its duties toward the teaching of freshmen, and one of my first concerns was to remind my colleagues that Freshman English was a departmental responsibility, and not a stepchild. They were open-minded and eventually persuadable, and they agreed to put their knowledge of rhetorical techniques to the test of elementary demonstration before freshmen. Though they were frequently unnerved by their students' inadequacies, they were always courageous and often impressively competent. A second concern—a wish to help create a climate in which college and high-school teachers of English could talk good-naturedly and directly—met with some rebuffs. The attack on the public-schools had made high-school teachers uneasy and suspicious, and my convictions about how composition should be taught were almost impossible to practice in the typically large and undisciplined classes of high schools. There were just too many students and too few properly trained English teachers. And the foolish pedagogy which thought the outside world should be duplicated in the classroom made it very difficult to maintain an environment of even lukewarm academic discipline in the public schools. Fortunately, the work of people like Dr. Conant centered public and college attention not merely on this problem, but also on its solution, so that now, I believe, we are beginning to come out of the educational wilderness (I prefer this word to "wasteland") that helped make Freshman English necessary in the first place, and hence created The Director of Freshman English—the director, incidentally, whose chief measure of merit is his success in making himself superfluous.

But this is a cliché, at least among administrators, and I really feel neither successful nor superfluous. Given the present degree of literacy in the average college-bound student, Freshman English is still a necessity, and the administrative machinery required to operate it is large and complex and constantly in need of attention and repair. For instance, the procedures for the testing, sorting and scheduling of thousands of students so that they end up in the right classrooms at the right time with the right instructors are so inextricably mixed that failure in one can create a total confusion. Students pile up in the hallways, instructors sit bewildered in empty classrooms, and all the phones ring complainingly at once. The director, who may be responsible for the situation in the first place—generally in the sense that he may have assumed students and instructors would follow his mimeographed directions—is the only one who can repair the situation. Having invented the machinery, he is the only one who knows how to uncrank it so that the gears mesh again. On the surface at least, it is not a noble function, and a sensitive director is always aware that he may be performing it largely because no one else wants to. He wonders too what his slavery to busyness is doing to his own soul: whether his energy that once seemed so limitless is now spreading itself over so much territory that it seems thin and watery, and irretrievable forever. But this is self-pity, and it kills. For myself, the charm of being an administrator is that it requires a sense of timing and detail that are conspicuous only when they are missing. And the sense of personal accomplishment comes from the attempt to learn and practice the patience, self-control, and the uncynical clear-sightedness about total effects that other people can afford to lack. His colleagues will always talk about high principles and frequently act like barbarians; but an administrator has to translate principle into policy, in an actual physical and human environment, and make it civil and workable. This is his challenge; the imagination and energy he brings to bear on his work represent his personal reaching for creativeness. This is the search that unites him with the teachers and writers and other discoverers who work around him, and this is why, everything considered, I think the job is worth doing.

University of Washington

. . . *From an Exile*

CHANDLER DAVIS

I AM NOT a professor. Maybe I never will be one.

My apprenticeship was honorable, as a teaching fellow at Harvard, where I got my Ph.D. in mathematics, and as an instructor at the University of Michigan. I loved the university life. Not that it occurred to me at the time to compare it to any other; I had never seriously considered leaving it.

However, it happened that one summer ten distinguished members of my faculty convened (five at a time) and unanimously declared me guilty of "deviousness, artfulness, and indirection hardly to be expected of a University colleague." I had refused, first before the House Committee on Un-American Activities and then before these juries of professors, to answer yes or no to the question, was I a Communist. The juries could assume (with that background and in the year 1954) that their recommendation that I be fired would mean my complete expulsion from the profession.

In fact my life as a mathematician, though attentuated, is not extinguished. I have managed to get a certain amount of research done. I show up at Math Society meetings. My fellow mathematicians, who stood up for me most gratifyingly when distinguished juries were telling them I was not fit for their company, still welcome me to their company. They gave me the pleasure and honor of a year's fellowship at the Institute for Advanced Study. Currently I have an editorial job with our reviewing journal—a position of, at any rate, responsibility.

But the universities—the universities of America have so far opened only their back door to me, only a crack, though I knocked at their front door, politely but unmistakably, for years.

So now under their window what song do I raise? A howl of grief? Have I risen to haunt you, displaying my shocking wounds to wrench your conscience? Not precisely.

To prove that I am fit to teach would be too easy to be interesting. I was exiled from academe, not as an incompetent, but as a heretic. To prove that my heresies meet your standards of tolerability or your dean's (though it might be difficult enough, all right) would be uninteresting because too special. There is a considerable fraternity of academic exiles these days, and there is no need to single me out from it.

I propose to give an account of the fraternity. Especially its admission procedures. I will ask you to consider what the exiles were and how they were removed from the universities; and exactly how easily they can be spared.

First, though, an evaluation in general of the dissenter's contribution to the university. This is the right decade for it. In a time when selection of academic personnel had been operating smoothly, the evaluation I mean to make might seem harmlessly truistic; today, my claims may seem tall claims indeed. The case for expelling the dissenter has been so much repeated recently; the notion that the dissenter is at any rate not important has offered such welcome consolation to the reluctant accessories to his expulsion; even the dissenter's defense has so often fallen back on the opportunistic argument that he is just like everyone else. I argue the importance of having colleagues who differ from you.

I

The dissenter's main contribution he makes only if his heresy is valid. Any university should aspire to recognize and encourage a modern Copernicus, in any field of thought. Recognition and encouragement might come too late if they waited for the innovation to be acknowledged correct by the department chairman (let alone the trustees).

This homily seems vulnerable when you think about it. If a truth is so obscure that we can't perceive it, we professors who are specialists in perceiving truths, then isn't the burden on its advocates to lick it into better shape? Why should they be granted academic rewards for a seedling theory, on credit against its eventual maturation?

Well, of course, the burden is on its advocates to advocate it. But in the nature of things a really significant innovation is likely to be hard to appreciate, or even understand, in the old terms. Its advocates themselves may not understand it too well. Their easily stated tenets may seem self-exposing falsehoods to normal people (particularly if they deny something economically or emotionally precious), and may, indeed, be wrong. The new generally resembles the old in one respect anyhow: not being perfect.

A valuable innovation may appear, yet its adherents remain an uncelebrated minority (even among the enlightened) for some time.

Furthermore it may need, more than an accepted doctrine, patient service by full-time acolytes. Not only because they will be better able to see its correctness; not only because their painstaking work can gather material for convincing the unconverted; but also because the main value of the innovation may *consist in* its application as a method of detailed analysis. What would the theory of evolution be today if there had nowhere been freedom to do anything more than *believe* it? It would still be, as in Erasmus Darwin's time, an intellectually attractive fancy. It became part of science only thanks to its rich elaboration in the nineteenth century.

Here I have to distinguish between the "amateur dissenter" who believes a heresy while making his living at an orthodox vocation, and the "professional dissenter" who devotes his main intellectual effort to the heresy. What I have been saying leads to the conclusion that the universities should welcome professional dissenters, even though some of them (one can't tell except in hindsight which ones) will turn out not to have had anything of distinctive value to contribute. This is so important that if at the moment no first-class candidates are on the market, the universities should welcome even somewhat dubious ones—just to advertise the existence of a demand for professional dissenters! The penalty for keeping these people around is small: at worst their heresy may be altogether wrong, but even in that unlikely extreme case it may, confronting truer competing ideas, help generate new and still truer ideas.

Does this mean embracing the angle-trisecting mathematician and the hollow-earth cosmologist? And if not, how can we draw the line? By what criterion should a department executive committee decide, among prospective appointees whose specialties seem absurd, which one to prefer? Should everyone competent to teach freshman courses become thereby the judge of the value of his own work?

The department should not, I would say, attempt to draw a boundary around the respectable portion of its field, maintaining within the boundary a "balanced department" in which rewards are dispensed even-handedly. This would lead to mechanical judgments where sensitive ones are called for. Let the department follow its own judgment as to where the greatest value lies. Let anyone adopting deviant standards resign himself to being judged by accepted ones, and accordingly expect to see himself somewhat underrated. Only let him be judged fairly and not resented. Thus A. M. Turing at Manchester—in the years before the economic importance of large digital computers made his interest in algorithms a widespread one—was accepted and respected for his excellence by standards other than his own, and supported in pursuing his lonely specialty. A less extraordinary talent might have been forced to switch to a fashionable specialty, and even Turing earned less respect than he gets in hindsight. But you can't hope to reward a man for being ahead of his time more highly than you reward the man who is on a wrong track when you can't tell them apart, so determine the amount of the reward by averaging the possibilities. Remember to be fairly generous in your guesswork: the number of beginning scholars is expected to increase fast, and more and more can be spared for the byways, if they're drawn to them.

All this pertains primarily to the professional dissenter. I suppose I am an amateur dissenter myself: most of my peculiar convictions, certainly including those I was fired for, have no tendency to reflect themselves in unconventional mathematics. Still I take them seriously—as, say, a Catholic may take God seriously although he is not a priest. Let me not understate the case for the amateur dissenter.

It is a strong one. If we desire to prepare the soil for an unpredicted innovation, we have no way of providing that it lies within one of the narrow plots which are the accepted disciplines. The innovation may attract disciples long before it is recognized as a possible way to make one's living: then it will *have* to begin as a hobby. Similarly, a new art form may be fun for its aficionados long before they dare to propose taking it seriously. In general, the universities can put up with much more fantastic deviation on the part of the amateur dissenter, because they lay no wager at all that he is right; having seen to it that he earns his keep, they can afford to leave his off hours up to him; thereby they are able to extend an invitation to progress further into the future.

Progress *is* the universities' business; their function is not merely custodial. And I maintain that just as innovations in ideas should be fostered in the universities more than outside, so should innovations in values. In some departments (literature and philosophy, at least) this is in the nature of the announced subject matter. But as a long-time lover of the bull session let me state the case more broadly. University students are a large group of active people, at the age for deciding what they want. Regardless of how material the subject matter of their specialty may be, they are concerned with values: they have to choose one goal for their lives above another. Their parents' choices may be, for them, wrong. They need, so that they can choose independently, an environment permissive toward the unexpected and rather charmed by it. To provide this environment is part of the universities' function; and one ingredient is professors who, while varying widely in their professional aspect, vary still more widely extracurricularly.

The universities *are* hotbeds of heresy. At least they

usually are; it is characteristic for them to be; they should be. They should be teeming with intellectual doctrines some of which the majority find useless or even false, and with moral doctrines some of which the majority find unattractive or even evil. And the diverse parties should dwell side by side, not with the tolerance of indifference, but embattled and cherishing each other: each should know that in its quest the contest with those who disagree will bring faster progress than would an unobstructed route.

The description does not fit the *status quo*. It does not ideally fit the *status quo ante* either. But if there is a shortage of active doctrinal challenge in the universities today, it is in order to give at least a brief, anxious look at the most conspicuous blow to academic freedom of recent years: political firings of professors.

II

The exiles, then. Who should I mean by "exile"? Those who were fired from university teaching jobs for their politics, surely, or forced to resign. But also it seems natural to include those who for the same cause simply were not able to find a job, or were obliged to accept jobs far below their qualifications, to accept non-academic jobs, or to emigrate. I will include anyone who qualified on any of these counts at any time during the current Red-hunt—say, from 1947 (Truman's first "loyalty" program) to 1959 (when I am writing).

We exiles have not been systematically studied. Eminent social scientists with foundation grants have studied academic freedom by surveying random samples of working professors (which, if it is not convenient wilful blindness, is at any rate a very different approach). One professor set out to write a book on the exiles, but became one before it was finished, which interfered seriously with its progress. We have been treated, sometimes misleadingly, by a few novelists.

What I can tell you in a few pages is told from knowledge (even though I have made no survey, and will cite few names). We exiles know each other pretty well—partly because some of us shared political contacts in the 'forties for which we were all punished subsequently, and partly because our shared predicament now draws us together.

To give you an idea—I sat down the other night and listed all the exiles I could think of. (I arbitrarily excluded people who lost their jobs by refusing to sign generally required oaths, as at the University of California, although a good many of them would qualify.) In about fifteen minutes I ran the list up to eighty! Not all the eighty are known to me by name, but thirty-seven of them I have met, and these include several of my close friends.

This is a good many exiles. Altogether there must be something between a hundred and a thousand—smaller, for illustration, than the number of women teaching in co-ed colleges, but much larger than the number of Negroes teaching in other than Negro colleges. Loss of a group this size is significant, at a time when universities are hard up for faculty; and some of the exiles are a good deal more than minimally competent.

But these sacrifices to the "loyalty" revival are far from a random sample. How were we selected?

Many were non-co-operators before Congressional committees. If such testimony was public, it was often followed, as in my case, by a strictly academic inquisition. These hearings provided a semblance of independence for the administration's eventual decision to fire; for, though caused by and roughly patterned after the Congressional ones, they were carried on by university people, often the victim's own colleagues. This very feature made them incomparably more painful. Of the two professors I can think of who went through such hearings in public universities *without* being fired, one quit anyhow, in disgust at the humiliating lack of confidence in him which the hearings expressed!

The majority of us became exiles more gently. An agent from the Un-American Committee or the F.B.I. would speak to a dean, who would then reach agreement with the fingered professor that it would be best for both parties if the firing was unpublicized. Or more gently yet—a thesis adviser would include in his letters of recommendation the hint that a fresh Ph.D. was "much concerned with social problems," and with or without further inquiry, employers would pass him by. Such practices are quite general. I know of instances among our mightiest private institutions. Unquestionably, since they are secret, there are many times as many instances as I know of; and it is reasonable to assume, by extrapolation, that still milder discrimination against left-wingers, carrying too light a sentence to make them exiles, must happen still oftener.

The whole gamut of methods continues in use, too. Several of the exiles joined us with full newspaper accompaniment within the last two years; and a number of professors have been convincingly threatened with exiling during 1959–60.

Many of the exiles succeeded in returning to academic status comparable to what they lost; but most have not. This story, well worth telling, I must skip.

What sort of people were exiled? In the first place, it should be understood that among them were Communists. I know it is cried that the Red-hunters aim at a much broader target than just the Communist Party; and most of them do seem to. But if one of them aims at a peace committee, say, his attack will get more co-operation if he can find a Communist in the committee on whom to concentrate it. I know it is cried that some of the Red-hunters are plain liars and that most of them will admit fantastic "evidence" in support of a charge of Communism; and this is true, too. But the standards of evidence in these cases, though shamefully low, were at any rate such that Communists were much more likely to be fired as Communists than anti-Communists were.

Along with the Communist, the exiles include many more people who, even to objective eyes, rather resemble Communists: former Communists, members of organizations which had Communist support, former members of such organizations, non-Communist Socialists, theoretical Marxists, etc. It makes sense to class most of these in a single group, and to say that, though mostly not Communists, they were accurately accused of the heresy of leftism; for they share certain ideological tendencies which the Red-hunters systematically attempt to suppress as "communistic." There are non-left-wing exiles who were accurately accused of such heresies as pacifism or (in the South) anti-segregationism, and exiles who were inaccurately accused of one heresy or another. But the non-left-wing exiles, however important, are not very numerous. For the sake of simplicity I will usually, from here on, discuss the exiles as if there were only the left-wing exiles, of which I am one.

My first conclusion is that not one of us (left-wing or other) should have been fired—indeed, indeed, that there was no *prima-facie* suspicion that any of us should be; hence that many distinguished juries not only arrived at wrong answers but concerned themselves with preposterous questions.

If Marxism was so crackpot a doctrine that it prevented sound scholarship, one might well investigate whether a colleague had contracted it. I have pointed out that the champion of an unrecognized doctrine must face some extra burden to establish his competence. But this is irrelevant here because the left-wing scholars I am talking about were not attacked by colleagues for professional unsoundness. Our competence was either unmentioned by our attackers or (as in my case) conceded.

We were accused of being under intellectual discipline which hindered open-mindedness. Now the fact is (I know these people, remember) that sure enough! some of us are almighty cocksure; some can irritate me even when I agree with what they're cocksure of. I have also known cocksure conservatives, but nobody has proposed that they be fired, much less that all conservatives be fired because some are cocksure. We exiles are not subject to a single discipline; the diversity of our opinions would surprise you; more to the point, we are most of us, I would say, a more independent, contentious and open-minded lot than the professors who survived us. But even if we were on the whole much more dogma-tied, this would be no call to single us out from the other dogmatists. Particularly since diehard adherence to a heresy is in general less menacing to free inquiry than matter-of-course adherence to orthodoxy: because the heretic, being constantly challenged, is deprived of the illusion that his rut is the whole road.

Then also, we were accused of influencing students. A shocking thought! Well-meaning friends sometimes defended us with pleas that, of course, we kept our poisonous ideas to ourselves. But to us, our left-wing ideas seem true, and therefore not poisonous. We would want to avoid putting undue pressure on our students to accept them, but not to avoid even submitting them to students! In practice most of us did go to the extreme of concealing our left-wing ideas from our students—but from realistic fear for our own security, not from fear of corrupting the students. Even if our views are all wrong, it would not corrupt any thinking person just to hear them advocated.

The professional dissenters among us had not merely the right to "influence" students, but the responsibility. A philosophy professor who accepts dialectical materialism, for instance, will have difficulty in speaking honestly if he tries to speak as a philosopher without speaking as a dialectical materialist. Herbert Phillips, in this predicament, set an example of courage and fairness to shame many of his fellow Marxists as well as his enemies: presenting various positions but avowing plainly which was his. The colleagues of such a man, if they think Marxism is not good philosophy, may then regret that their Marxist is not too good a philosopher, and think to improve him by converting him; but they should remember that it will not improve him to intimidate him into donning Thomism or empiricism.

We amateur dissenters had it easier. Our only real responsibility in this regard was to avoid wasting class time on irrelevant expositions of our heresies. Most of us held to this scrupulously; perhaps if the incentive of fear had been absent, we might have produced more counterparts of those conservative colleagues who larded their lectures with irrelevant anti-W.P.A. or anti-Soviet jokes.

Then, too, we were accused of belonging to a conspiracy

to commit espionage or armed revolution. A very few were actually accused of spying; but almost all of us were not, I think, even suspected of overt acts of this nature. What was the accusation, then? Merely that we supported organizations which somewhere and sometime engaged in espionage or furthered revolutions? This charge was true of some of us. A telling charge, perhaps—if it had been brought, say, by our pacifist colleagues. But a laughable charge when brought by people who consider the professor's role perfectly consistent with supporting espionage by the C.I.A. and revolution in Guatemala.

I am not saying that Russian power politics and American power politics are mirror twins, but only that the university should not be an agent of either. It should be impartial on matters where individuals, or even the freest state, can not be impartial. However anti-Soviet some of you are, however strongly you suspect foul treason among us, you should not involve the university in fighting that non-academic battle. Counterespionage is not the dean's job. He's probably not much good at it anyway.

I'm afraid I have been belaboring the obvious for a couple of pages now. The standard rationalizations for firing Reds have the transparency of the emperor's new clothes. They are never invoked against conservatives, though logically applicable; they are rarely bothered with in the quiet firings. I can't believe that such poppycock persuaded many of our colleagues that we deserved exile. I do believe that many of our colleagues were persuaded, by seeing the poppycock most solemnly received, that they could not afford to defend us.

The only essential charge against us was heresy. From outside the universities came a clamor to dress the anti-

Communist ranks; we were charged with being out of line. To fire us for this was wrong.

But I said it was wrong in every single case. Do I really mean to be so sweeping? Surely there were *some* incompetents among those fired? Quite likely, by chance, a few; but none, I dare say, whose incompetence was proved in the course of deciding to fire them for heresy. But surely there were some cases of political immorality? Particularly, people who falsely denied that they were Communists? Yes, a few; it saddens me that some people diminished themselves by lying in an effort to save their positions; but I remember that the test they failed most of their colleagues did not face; I think of the far more numerous people, now snug in their academic tenure, who began much earlier in response to much less severe threats to conceal and even suppress their own dangerous thoughts; and I think of Galileo; and I decide that the universities, and morality, would be best served by a lenient view of forced recantations.

My second main conclusion about the left-wing exiles is that we do not now constitute a thriving heresy. What has been banished from the campuses in us is a collection of rather like-minded individuals, not a coherent ideological movement. For agreement on political and economic matters we may turn to each other, but for interesting new contributions we turn to the universities. We have the numbers and the talent to provide the nucleus of an intellectually creative heresy—why don't we?

(1) Being exiled has hurt our output. Unaccustomed jobs, emotional stress, separation from scholarly surroundings —it is hard to keep plugging. But a lot of us do.

(2) Too few of us are professional dissenters, too many amateurs. Maybe this is because full-time left-wing intellec-

tuals were already largely excluded from universities at the beginning of the period 1947–1959 (witness, *e.g.*, Scott Nearing, Morris U. Schappes and Paul Sweezy), and throughout the period faced much higher barriers. Radical students felt a bread-and-butter pull toward politically neutral vocations.

(3) We lack the sectarian spirit. I have mentioned that our opinions vary widely, but I am now making a different point. Even considering only left-wingers of some single species, a left-wing mathematician has closer affinity to a conservative mathematician, in many respects, than he has to a left-wing sculptor or lawyer. Well, naturally. But this is becoming more and more the case, during the decades of suppression of the left, because we left-wingers as individuals choose to make it so. We do not accept the fate of a pariah group. Most of us yearn for the masses, for the mainstream; and lack the patience to guard a peculiar flame through generations of persecution. (Contrast the pacifists!)

(4) I must add that a healthy school of Marxist thought in the Communist countries, if there was one, might be a valuable stimulus to American left-wing thought. A serious Marxist tradition does survive in those countries, but elevation to the status of official doctrine has not helped it: it has been entangled with governmental expediencies, and most enfeebling of all, it has been deprived of confrontation by active dissenters. *Caveat victor.*

III

My friend E. E. Moise (a tolerable maverick, no exile) remarked while the political purges were in full swing that the universities would not suffer if the victims were simultaneously and mysteriously to disappear, but would suffer seriously from the act of firing them. He should not be held to account for literal interpretation of his rhetorical statement. I have pointed out that losing our services was not a negligible loss quantitatively. I would demur more strongly that the loss of a healthy heresy is much more serious than the loss of so many individual scholars; and though I have confessed that we can't claim to be a thriving heresy today, we might be if we hadn't taken such a beating. The ideas we were prevented from developing may not all be developed by the unpurged, who lack our odd slant.

But let me get to the point of Moise's remark. We were not pruned hygienically from the academic tree but wrenched from it in violation of its orderly growth. It should be inspected for damage.

Most obvious (though not most important), and most obviously intended by the Red-hunters, is the demoralization of the unexiled left. The lesson that they'd better watch their step or they may be next, is too obvious to be ignored. Those who have not in the past approached the left, are likewise well taught that they had better not. This, as much as the failings of the exiles, accounts for the recent decline in the left-wing intellectual movement or movements. Thousands of professors are revisiting conservatism this season, and I wonder how many of them would have been impelled to make the tour by its intrinsic charm.

A more general lesson has been taught, perhaps less consciously. It has been demonstrated that the universities cannot afford to shield a few faculty members if it means hurting the whole institution by jeopardizing bequests (this is dean's talk; a pamphleteer would say equipollently, the universities sacrifice academic freedom to the big money). In the long run this is ominous; even immediately it may occasion perfectly realistic uneasiness in any professor, his administration being what administrations are today. Your job security is rightly envied, professors, but it is contingent on your not irritating too far (even unintentionally) too many rich.

In this direction are grave effects of the purges. But how far do they go?

In the social sciences, certain types of research motivated by Marxist or related theories, are discouraged. But far from abandoned! In sociology particularly, the development of the previously active lines of research, even apparently "dangerous" ones, has been thwarted gratifyingly little. (So, at least, I gather from rumors reaching me; I speak as an outsider to the field.) This is partly because some people are courageous; partly because the dangerousness of an idea can be camouflaged sometimes by jargon; partly because a line of research previously pursued by two hundred investigators may lose half of those without being fatally undermanned.

Gross stifling of research has resulted here and there from the firings, but only in fields obviously related to the Communist Party or to current governmental policy.

(I want to mention in passing the proliferation of social-scientific work frankly and more or less directly in the service of current governmental policy. I have suspicions that these government-screened political scientists are taking over from the more academic thinkers in their departments by force of numbers; that opposition to the trend has been deterred by the sacrosanctity of the Established Economic System and the Bipartisan Foreign Policy; that this sacrosanctity, on the campus, owes much to the firings. This is perhaps an instance, not of gross stifling, but of gross imbalance.)

The subtle inhibitions are more widespread. I call them

subtle, but only in the sense that they're petty and pass without much notice—not in the sense that they're sophisticated. They act in little spasmodic avoidances. A professor recoils from discussing economic influences on ideology; or from detecting a pecuniary motive in the policies of a corporation president or diplomat; or from publishing an appreciation of Sean O'Casey unredeemed by a peck at his politics. Poor timid thing! You can nibble the edge of one of our ideas without obligation to accept the whole cake! But the timid things are not tempted, and circle far around. These automatic avoidances are so taken for granted that they have been made the basis of a familiar polemic technique: one sketches wittily an analogy between a Communist slogan and the formulation of one's opponent—the latter being thereby demolished without the trouble of refuting it. The response to this technique's effectiveness, in turn, is for formulations vulnerable to it to be suppressed in advance by their author even if there is no genuine similarity to anything left-wing at all.

Left-wing ideas are being stamped out, but by a terribly broad boot.

The subtle inhibitions are pervasive, but not omnipresent. Do they act against boldness of invention in fields far from politics? I have been observing mathematicians, and, less extensively, physicists, throughout these years. As far as they go, I venture a definite answer: No. Limitation in social thinking has not caused limitation of invention in general. I can conceive of such a relationship, but so far I have not observed it.

And I venture to favor, among possible explanations, this as the main one: Even in social thinking, *the heresy-hunt does not punish originality* per se, and is not perceived as threatening originality. At the instant of conception or even of first public expression, an idea is not "dangerous." The thought-controllers are afraid only of organized heresy; likewise for scapegoat purposes an organized heresy is most attractive; and an organized heresy probably has a stabilized core of doctrine. Its adherents take the doctrine as basis for their further thinking; whether or not they take it as the exclusive basis, they may proceed to thinking of brilliance and daring, or of utter passive repetition. This will not decide their punishment. To the extent that they are punished for their ideas, it will be for their acceptance of the basic doctrine, which is not original with any of them. If the doctrine is by and large true, then the heresy-hunt will have punished wisdom, but not originality.

Of course a successful heresy-hunt, once it has dispersed organized heresy, may turn to striking at anything unexpected. Then, indeed, *all* experimenting with ideas is risky, and if one is to survive, one's protective inhibitions must be more confining. The governmental "loyalty-security" programs have no doubt entered this stage; but the university aspect of the Red-hunt, my subject here, has not.

And suppose it never does. And suppose that the general paralysis infects the universities no worse than it has. And suppose that the exiles become no less dispensable than now and not much more numerous. Can you then consider the episode closed, speak of McCarthyism (and of us) in the past tense, and relax in the knowledge that your universities are fairly free (at least for everybody but the exiles, who weren't perfect anyway)?

This is the general view. Opposition to a firing is rapidly engulfed, once the firing is concluded, by impatience to forget about it. One of the distinguished colleagues who found me fireable was elected president of the local A.A.U.P. chapter less than two years later (while the national A.A.U.P. was still in process of duly censuring my firing). Almost no administrations guilty of excluding teachers for their politics have reversed themselves. Exceptions: a very few quietly excluded scholars have subsequently been just as quietly admitted; several University of California non-signers were reinstated, of course; and there was one college which pretty explicitly repudiated a political firing quite like mine, though without offering the victim his job back. One of my friends said fervently that he would not want me to get my job back, it would be too unpleasant for everybody concerned. Unpleasant—that I grant. Most of the exiles have made it easier for the academic world to forget them by dropping out of sight to avoid unpleasantness and to avoid drawing more fire.

But it won't do. For your own sake, for the universities' sake, you must face what happened. More than you need the exiles in particular, you need dissent in general, a profusion of ideas richer than you have seen before. You must welcome dissent; you must welcome serious, systematic, proselytizing dissent—not only the playful, the fitful, or the eclectic; you must value it enough, not merely to refrain from expelling it yourselves, but to refuse to have it torn from you by outsiders. You must welcome dissent, not in a whisper when alone, but publicly so potential dissenters can hear you.

What potential dissenters see now is that you accept an academic world from which we are excluded for our thoughts. This is a manifest signpost over all your arches, telling them: Think at your peril. You must not let it stand. You must (defying outside power; gritting your teeth as we grit ours) take us back.

. . . *Say Something Nasty about Pittsburgh!*

EDWARD ECHOLS

IN AN essay concerned with the laggard progress of a lecture tour across the United States, Stephen Leacock describes the massive indifference of potential audiences to his offerings until, in an interview in Chicago, he happened to repeat several of the standard uncomplimentary clichés about the Windy City in its Gangster Era. When these were reported sensationally in the Chicago press, the success of his local appearances was solidly assured, so much so that when he began his eastward return, his agent sent off a wire somewhat to this effect: "Say something nasty about Pittsburgh!"

Of late, it has become both commonplace and profitable to "say something nasty about education." These attacks, in general, derive from one of two sources: from those forced to deal with the products of present-day education, who find them wanting, and say so, vehemently and articulately; and from those who, though themselves identified with the field, divorce themselves from the group they attack (*i.e.*, the Educators *vs.* the Educationists) and thus manage, in theory, to avoid a charge of masochistic fouling of their own rather comfortable nest.

It is not often that one in Education is afforded an opportunity to examine the causes and effects that have placed him where he is at the moment. Such auto-analysis is entirely justified if it does nothing more than clarify just precisely where one *is* at the moment.

Since no attack is so bitter as that of the duped and disillusioned, confession literature, on all levels, consistently enjoys great popularity in our couch-conscious society; these confessions follow a reasonably predictable pattern of youthful bedazzlement, mature disillusion, and a resultant regeneration that is frequently lyrically evangelical. I can recall being early cynically impressed by the Southern brand of traveling evangelist; these gentlemen, I thought, had pursued a lengthy career of fleshly pleasure and only after they had burned themselves out, so to speak, did they dedicate themselves to warning others away from the activities which seemed to offer such a delightful contrast to their present situation. In assessing one's own pursuits, it is thus well to be careful in pointing a moral; you may irresistibly lure those whom you are attempting to save. As an ex-college teacher and an ex-Southern(er) college teacher, I find myself with not one, but *two* possible areas for confession and evangelism. But, to borrow Southern idiom, as an ex-college teacher, I am by no means "Reconstructed"; as an ex-Southerner, however, I am at the moment very much in danger of being "Reconstructed," at long last.

One can, in the final analysis, hardly avoid the twin pressures of heredity and environment, especially in the South, where heredity has always been of great moment. Here, lawyers tend to beget lawyers, doctors, doctors, or, at the least, professional men, professional men. Heredity I can, except in the broadest implication, rule out. My family is undistinguished, if seventeenth-century, Virginian; in a state where, by this time, virtually every family is in some measure related, my connections with early Virginia Men of Distinction are remote, the consequence unidentifiable. After The War, my forebears lived in reasonably genteel poverty on inherited land, too proud or too tired to work, until, at last, my father's generation was compelled to seek non-agrarian employment in a dormant economy. In a display of pioneer spirit somewhat unseemly in native Virginians, my father and mother moved westward to Oregon, but Virginia ties and Virginia identification were so uxorially powerful that my family, including now my brother and myself, returned once more to the Old Dominion. This colossally expensive move forced my father to start all over again, this time in West Virginia, where he became superintendent of a coal mine in a small, company-owned village on a creek in a valley so steep-sided that the sun appeared daily not before nine o'clock and disappeared by four on even the longest day of the year.

I spent ten years in this place, enjoying a position of privilege modest by extern standards, absolute at the local level. My father, whose formal education was slight, but whose concern with education was great, was instrumental in organizing the local school on a permanent basis. At the school, my brother and I were the star performers, chiefly because only for us was there a chance that formal education might ultimately prove of value.

Even in these unlikely surroundings—a narrow, creek-cut valley fifteen miles long containing twenty or so mines and villages—there existed a kind of aristocracy. A number of the mines were privately owned and operated, and the owners, men of considerable wealth, lived each in his own village. It was, in a sense, the old plantation system transferred to the most unlikely surroundings. The aristocracy, which included the superintendents representing the large mining companies, were entirely "expatriate"; the men who worked the mines were the local "natives." Looking back, I would say that the impressive bridge parties of the ladies were the equivalent of the well-known custom of "dressing for dinner in the jungle." We children also enjoyed the advantages of the privileged class; we played with the "native" children, had them in the house, occasionally shared their head lice, but the social levels were clear-cut and impossible of violation. In most of these early years, Negroes played no part; not until the Great Strike of the early 'twenties did my father bring in the first train-load, under guard, as strikebreakers. For him, and thus for us, the status of these Negroes was that of Old Virginia; we even had the usual "house" Negroes: Uncle Dave, who taught us to ride a horse; Sam, the house boy and chauffeur, who was carried into the living room one night, shot in the stomach, and sent thirty miles by special train—engine and caboose at midnight—to die in a hospital, a striking example of the old benevolent ante bellum relationship.

So these "best people," my parents among them, endured their existence in exile, discharging their duty in this outpost of "empire," looking forward to an ultimate return to Virginia.

For us, the opportunity came with the sudden death of my father, on the eve of the collapse of local bituminous mining and the depression. Within three months, we were settled in Charlottesville, ostensibly under the aegis of a cousin-professor at the University of Virginia, my mother now involved in that common economic retreat of the Southern gentlelady, the "keeping" of students. The Great Depression, however, soon dispelled any hope that this enterprise would provide, as an additional bonus, a university education for my brother and myself. He managed two years, I, one, before we were finally liquidated.

It is a curious fact that in this period of financial touch and go, with no fixed assets and no prospects of same, neither of us considered for a moment any "practical" course of study. We were dedicated to the cause of the humanities, inheritors of the long Southern tradition of humanistic education. This decision may also have represented a deliberate withdrawal from reality; in an era in which no course of training could guarantee a job, it must be admitted that there was as much demand for a philosopher as for a steamfitter. In any event, we stood, unshaken, by the inherited tradition.

The New Deal, the timely repeal of Prohibition, and an uncle, in ascending order of importance, resulted in a personal prosperity quite uncommon for the 'thirties. My brother now managed a Ph.D. in the marvelously impractical field of Germanic Philology. I returned to the university, finally, with the somewhat more practical aim of a degree in architecture, but, finding my architectural techniques somewhat lacking in finesse, turned, in conscious withdrawal from reality, I now suspect, to that most aristocratic of Southern intellectual pursuits—the Classics.

Historically, all education in the South has been aristocratic. I suspect that Mr. Jefferson's ideas of education did not differ markedly from his ideas of government; in the final analysis, both were for the "best people." The continued aristocratic nature of Southern higher education has been, until recently, occasioned by the generally low standards of Southern primary and secondary education, the lack of opportunity for "trade school" graduates, and, no doubt as a result of the strong European bias of the ante bellum South, confidence in the British concept of an identical general education as preparation for any particular job. In the postwar period, when many of the old and cherished class distinctions disappeared, education—specifically, the holding of a degree from one of the distinguished Southern institutions—became a unique and not easily won status-symbol. This sudden subversion of all the familiar class-distinction symbols, no doubt to some extent vindictive, on the part of the determinedly classless North, led the upper-class South to place even greater emphasis upon education. The old tradition of privileged position was much too strong to support any spirit of class emancipation through universal education. Fortunately for this point of view, there was little interest in general education from any source; in a South basically concerned with the problems of material recovery, general education must have seemed an expensive luxury; in most of the South, it still does.

So Southern education managed to remain aristocratic on all levels; denied status-by-wealth, the "best people" continued to enter those fields requiring extensive training. The postwar Southern aristocracy thus continued to be birth-and-education based; only wealth had, in most instances, been eliminated.

To be truly aristocratic, education should be unfunctional; in some countries, primogeniture and the convenient inheritance-from-a-maiden-aunt make it possible for those of gentle birth to devote a productive lifetime to a study of the Latin ablative case. So study for admission to the professions must, in the scale of such things, rank below the pure Humanities. Changing economic conditions, however, have tended to all but eliminate those for whom education bears no relation to livelihood; today even the Humanities are pursued by those who must, in the final analysis, make a living from the Humanities. It is this necessity which has contributed to the recent growth of liberal-arts colleges; there seems a definite trend toward the expansion of teachers' colleges and religious colleges into degree-granting liberal-arts institutions.

College teaching in the South has always enjoyed great social prestige. Colleges and universities have been manned, faculty and students, by successive generations of people of privilege. This pattern of succession, often bordering upon frank nepotism, has tended to inhibit and to introvert Southern education; and it is powerfully abetted by another widespread phenomenon, the strong religious feeling which has for years served the South as a substitute for general education. Religious pressure—official in the denominational schools, unofficial, but little less powerful, in the secular institutions —has tended always to hamper and handicap the seeker after other than the Southern brand of truth. The influence of religion on Southern education is furthered by the practice common in many institutions of making generous scholarship aid available to the sons of ministers. These men are numerous in college teaching, where often they devote themselves, with religious zeal, to secular congregations. And sometimes they are the best teachers.

For the pre-World War II student in the South, the types of institutions existent were somewhat limited. The best-known and most-sought-after were the old, aristocratic ante bellum schools, frequently forward-looking, just as frequently ultra-conservative. Many of the state universities belonged to this class, among them some of the South's most illustrious schools. The "Mechanical and Agricultural" colleges had not yet begun their spectacular post-Late War expansion, to meet the mushrooming demands of the new industrialized South. Last on the list were the church schools, running the gamut from the solidly distinguished to the frighteningly sectarian, biased, self-satisfied; it is among these schools supported by the myriad splinter-sects of the old non-aristocratic Southern denominations that originated the apocryphal(?) belief that the Bible was handed down in English.

Since I was living in a university town in a crippling depression, I was destined for the University of Virginia or nothing. I also attended secondary school in the university town; here I met for the first time personally the caste-status assumed by university teachers. During the 'thirties, financial limitations very likely kept more sons of professors in the public schools than might ordinarily have been the case. They tended to form a closed corporation, membership in which was virtually blocked for those of us on the fringes of the university. It may or may not be significant that the one friend I had in the university group was the son of a Professor of Education!

In spite of their, by my standards, assured position, they were vulnerable in matters academic, and I suspect that the challenge to beat these intellectual F.F.V.'s in this area reinforced my already more than casual interest in the pursuit of knowledge. Insofar as class standing was concerned, I was successful, but it was immediately obvious that, whereas a university career was for them a matter of course, for me it was to be a small scholarship and a losing financial battle, as I plodded unrealistically along the Academic Way.

In four grueling years of working for a living, I apparently learned nothing about the economic facts of the academic life. I could even misinterpret the obvious to support my choice; when I noted that the professor of Greek was teaching a total of seven students, it apparently did not occur to me that this represented the dying phase of a distinguished academic tradition. It simply impressed me as an uncrowded field in which to operate. And so I dedicated myself to a course that offered every opportunity for absolute financial disaster—the Lorelei pursuit of the Classics.

I managed a shaky M.A. in the early years of World War II. After the war, following several unrealistic escapist efforts, I was caught up in the lucrative deluge of service students responsible for the rapid and wholesale postwar expansion of all institutions of higher learning. In the immediate postwar reaction against the "How To . . ." curriculum and the veterans' seemingly deep-seated interest in the "Why" courses, the Humanities enjoyed a vigorous renascence, in which the Classics shared.

When the successive waves of migrating students, denied admission to their local colleges, reached the Deep South, the colleges hurriedly expanded their staffs, giving preference, in the main, to Southerners. Since native teachers were not available in sufficient numbers, Northerners were imported to beef up staffs formed in the nepotic 'twenties and 'thirties, when local graduates were hired in a benevolent inbreeding which occasionally produced some startling academic "sports." These veteran students and Northern faculty members brought a refreshing breath of air to the Humanities especially, to courses long held to be the private domain of the lazy, the curious, the droll and the confused. (I recall with special pleasure a Home Economics major who for one day elected Beginning Greek because "she had so many Greek friends in Mobile.")

I taught Latin, Greek and odd related courses at the University of Alabama for eight years, with results that were both satisfying and frustrating, the normal range. When it was evident that government support was not to be permanent, the students turned, of necessity, back to the "How To . . ." courses, leaving the Humanities to renew their old fight for survival. In co-educational institutions, however, there exists a built-in defense against the "How To . . ." courses—the co-eds themselves. If one's interest in higher education is largely other than intellectual (marriage, for instance), it is, curiously enough, less immediately obvious in the Humanities courses. In the field of Classics, for example, if the basic courses fail to draw the minimum quota of students, there is literally no end to the possible proliferation of material when it is a matter of survival, personal and departmental. Eventually, however, co-ed subsidization is not enough, and dwindling classes bring the Humanities once more under heavy fire from close-pocketed pragmatists. Not only Latin and Greek, but modern languages, history, even English were driven to the defensive, forced, like the Classics, to divide to conquer—English for Engineers (Who needs Dickens in the Andes?); Easy Physics for Home Economists, as opposed to Hard Physics for Physicists; Woodworking for Athletes, as opposed to Woodworking for Woodworkers. In short, we heralded the era of the Cafeteria Curriculum, where it was the spectacular, the artful and the decorated desserts which caught the fancy of the unsophisticated student and left him, at the final reckoning, intellectually flabby and outrageously short-changed. In some cases, the situation was effectively remedied when large companies, caught in the crisis of the cold war, began to stock-pile graduates against the possible outbreak of hostilities; elaborate on-the-job training programs trimmed the accumulated academic fat from the trainees and rendered them economically efficient.

In spite of association with a department that managed exceedingly well during this critical time for the Humanities,

I was at last forced to face the economic facts of academic life. It was at this time that the president, passing a young instructor on the campus, complained to a companion: "Don't we pay that man enough for him to get his hair cut?" No one would tell him the truth. This is the same president who, when presented with a request for additional instructors from one of the "practical" departments, authorized the hiring of two instructors at one thousand dollars a year less than the beginning salary of graduates of that department who entered other fields. I also recall being told with considerable satisfaction by the minister of one of the local deviate sects, who regularly brought me his themes for suggestions and corrections, that he was not only paid more than a university professor but was provided a furnished house and foodstuffs in addition! He was not the minister who lectured the student body at length under the sizzling Alabama sun on eschewing pleasures of the flesh, while sweat visibly drenched his linen-draped three hundred pounds of too, too solid flesh.

The typical college salary represents a beautifully honed compromise; it is a sum deemed sufficiently large to encourage, but not so large as to devitalize. Compensating for the mutually admitted inadequate financial return, however, are the fringe benefits: social prestige, a high degree of job security, dominance by right of position, and, perhaps most important, a compulsion to proselytize, especially evident in the Humanistic areas. For many, however, the perennial adverse differential in one's relationship to the world's goods finally dictates a change; and so it was with me.

In an area in which so many strive for so little, the dedicated educator trainee can look for very generous financial support from large foundations richly endowed for this purpose. The generally recognized backward nature of Southern education has long been of great concern to these foundations, and substantial aid is available to Southern educators willing to venture forth, usually north of the Mason and Dixon, for intellectual enlightenment and augmentation. These fellowships have, at times, proved a mixed blessing, for they open to the recipients of such largesse vistas of college teaching undreamed of in their native habitat. Consequently, it is considered necessary to insert in the terms of the grant a retaining clause to guarantee the return of the grantee to his college of origin. It is equally a tribute to the ability of many Southern teachers that Northern institutions dangle before them offers that are, by average Southern standards, dazzling, indeed. Often, for the first time, the Southern teacher realizes that it is possible to live on educational pay.

But most important and most significant, he may also learn that it is possible to live a normal life in what are, to him, integrated schools. The specter of integration, with all its implications, is yet another cross which the Southern teacher must somehow, by acceptable compromise, learn to bear. It is in this aspect of Southern *mores* that every semblance of rationalism is summarily abandoned; friendship, blood ties, even the fabled Code of the Southern Gentleman, in short, *nothing* (not even the Law!) functions in the face of integration.

The first and most obvious schism is geographical, and here, it must be admitted, the Northern attack is as absurd and illogical as the Southern defense. The Southerner, however, once the absurdities of North *vs.* South have been exhausted, is driven from one position to another, fighting a spirited rear-guard action, until he reaches finally the ultimate in rational travesty—the religious "proofs" cited in support of segregation. In this controversy, which he can in no way avoid if he elects to remain in the South, the educator frequently finds himself in an ambivalent position: he must be both rational and a Southerner, a by no means easy combination. His educator's rational intellect tells him that segregation is *per se,* on all grounds, untenable and indefensible; his emotions, his inheritance, sadly tell him that, in the final analysis, he is Southerner first and rational second. Fortunately for the South, there are men of good will who elect to stand and fight; but it was a sad experience to be, quite by accident, close to one of the South's most distinguished educators at one of the South's most notorious integration incidents and hear him say, as he turned to leave, the situation unresolved: "I guess they don't want me here." It was a prophetic statement. It was at this moment, I think, that I made my decision to leave the South. Needless to say, my loss is far greater than hers. I can never hope completely to eradicate the guilt; I can only, with thousands of others, learn to live with it, uneasily.

It is impossible for me to assess my motives for turning from college teaching to preparatory-school teaching without leaving myself open to a charge of "Sour Grapes"! Let us agree at the outset that since I do not hold a Ph.D., my value to a college, especially in a field like the Classics, is definitely and permanently limited. Once our mutual teeth are back off edge, however, I should like to undertake as objective an evaluation as possible of the reasons and results for my shift of theater of operations.

As the result of the demonstrated proof of Soviet intellectual (*i.e.,* scientific) progress, education on all levels has recently been subjected to close critical scrutiny, and there is one school of thought which would put the blame for the state of American affairs squarely at the wide and long-suffering door of American secondary-school education. It is futile to suggest that if we are in danger of coming in second in this contest of intellects, the fault must of necessity lie largely with that generation which presumably enjoyed the advantages of the legendary pre-Dewey, "tough" brand of education, a wholesale return to which, it is alleged, would put us out in front in the current brains' race. This strikes me as pure, self-deluding malarkey. Ideas are no respecter of persons or nations; education *en masse* produces many teachers of philosophy, but few philosophers, many Masters of Music, but few composers, etc., etc. No system can guarantee to produce genius to order; the best we can do is to try to develop some method of recognizing genius and to offer it adequate standards of training. Genius cannot be developed, but it can be trained. As a recent cartoon put it—it isn't enough simply to be a genius; you must be a genius *at* something!

In their disappointment at the "failure" of modern methods of education to achieve what are generally considered desirable results, many parents have sanctioned and supported a return to the framework of the nineteenth-century Classical Education. This system, with its emphasis upon Latin, Greek, mathematics, the *fundamentals,* produced, it is argued, men who distinguished themselves in a wide variety of fields. It is not too much to suggest, I think, that these men achieved distinction not directly as a result of their course of study (they had no choice!) but rather because they were men who, with their native brilliance, would have won distinction under any circumstances. Still and all, I am personally convinced that the study of "tough" subjects fashions an intellectual framework which does enable the student to move from the general to the particular with both ease and success.

If I did not believe this, I would find it difficult to defend the extensive study of Latin.

It is in the old, established private secondary schools that this concept of "Classical" education is most closely followed today; in a respectable number, the study of Latin is still compulsory. It is only natural then, in this age of "togetherness," that many classicists are willing to abandon the one-man-department isolation of college teaching for the large departments to be found in many prep schools. In many colleges, the Classics Department has been for many years the personal property of an aging professor with tenure; if he cannot be moved efficiently into administration—and the proportion of classicists in administrative posts *seems* very high—then the department is allowed to wither and decay until the old classicist, like the old soldier, fades away. If conditions warrant replacing the old campaigner, then the administrative anomaly of an assistant professor as department head results—an uncomfortable situation all around. By contrast, at Exeter at the moment, Latin is an eight-man department; this results in a cozy camaraderie unusual in college classical circles.

It is, of course, no longer necessary in prep-school circles to teach purely for altruistic motives. It is a matter of record that in 1959 a foundation endowment enabled a number of prep schools to establish endowed chairs averaging twelve thousand dollars' annual income.

One of the immediately appealing aspects of private-school teaching is the high degree of selectivity common in admissions policies. The "prestige" prep schools have always been vulnerable to a charge of social aristocracy. Well aware of this, many of these schools have instituted programs designed to substitute for the old aristocracy of class an aristocracy of intellect. Candidates, are screened, quite literally on a wholesale basis, and extensive scholarship aid is extended to those who are thought to meet the demands. It would be too much to expect that all those admitted are superior, or that top-flight students are not missed. Many high schools, operating on completely "democratic" principles, consistently produce outstanding students.

Granting the intellectually selective nature of his students, the prep-school teacher must, of course, adjust to the inequality in maturity between the prep school and the college student. Yet even here there is an overlap; it would be fair to say, on the basis of ever-increasing admissions to college with advanced standing, that many prep-school boys operate on a level of intellectual maturity superior to that of their college counterparts. Contrast the prep-school boy admitted with full sophomore standing to the inmates of the "sub-human" courses in English and mathematics which are an accepted part of the curriculum at many of the best universities.

On the debit side must be placed the obviously greater demand upon the hour-by-hour, day-by-day time of the preparatory-school teacher. These activities tend to lessen the intellectual productivity of the *average* prep-school teacher, but if the prep-school *teacher* be compared in this matter with the college *teacher,* I suspect that there is little to choose between them in total output.

It is difficult to assess accurately the relative general prestige of the prep-school teacher and the college teacher. In the final analysis, it depends largely upon the prestige of the institution. In the national "status-scale," however, I rather suspect that the college teacher *per se* takes precedence over his preparatory-school colleagues. This is a matter of tradition, of the ultimate outranking the contributor.

But it is, in my opinion, in this matter of "contributing"

that preparatory-school teaching offers the great satisfaction. One of the great burdens which the teacher, especially of the Humanities, on the college level must bear is the absolute impossibility of assessing with any accuracy the direct results of his efforts. He teaches year after year into a void, often the only tangible result of his work some casual word of appreciation expressed twenty years late by a returning old grad. By contrast, the preparatory-school teacher can often evaluate, in IBM terms, the success or failure of his teaching. For admission to college, the taking of the Advanced Placement Tests is virtually obligatory today; these tests are graded on a basis of 800 for "perfection." Even before the boy leaves the class, the teacher is able to measure accurately the effectiveness of his efforts. The college teacher, on the other hand, must learn to enjoy the lonely realm of terminal teaching; the preparatory teacher, susceptible to accurate extern- and self-appraisal, is equipped with a possible source of immense satisfaction.

It is, of course, entirely in the Classical Tradition for the classicist to associate himself with an Academy. The original Academy, founded by Plato, was located appropriately in a pleasure garden in Athenian suburbs. Here for more than eight hundred years, scholars sought for Truth. Cicero says of the Old Academy: "Their writings and methods contain all liberal learning, all history, all polite discourse; and besides they embrace such a variety of arts that no one can undertake any noble career without their aid. . . ." However, imperfectly they and we achieve such noble aims, the game is eminently worth the candle. *Vivat Academia!*

Phillips Exeter Academy